Working Memory
and Severe
Learning Difficulties

Working Memory and Severe Learning Difficulties

Charles Hulme

and

Susie Mackenzie

*Department of Psychology,
University of York U.K.*

 LAWRENCE ERLBAUM ASSOCIATES, PUBLISHERS
Hove (UK)   Hillsdale (USA)

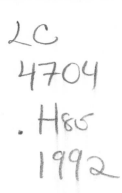
Lawrence Erlbaum Associates Ltd., Publishers
27 Palmeira Mansions
Church Road
Hove
East Sussex BN3 2FA
U.K.

British Library Cataloguing in Publication Data

Hulme, Charles
   Working memory and severe learning difficulties.–
   Essays in cognitive psychology. ISSN 0959-4779)
   I. Title. II. Mackenzie, Susie III. Series
   155.412

   ISBN: 0-86377-075-4

The text in this book was produced direct from disks supplied by the authors, via a
desk-top publishing system. Printed and bound by BPCC Wheatons Ltd., Exeter

Contents

Acknowledgements

This book has benefited from the help given to us by many people. First and foremost we should like to thank all the people (children and adults) who participated in our experiments. In particular, our thanks go to the staff and pupils of the following schools and Training Centres: Tang Hall, Knavesmire, Lidgett Grove, and Galtres Schools, York; Two Dales School, Leeds; Hebdon Rise, and Yearsley Bridge, Adult Training Centres, York. Our special thanks go to Chris Stevens, Headteacher of Galtres School for his enthusiastic support of the research and for taking on board how short-term memory problems may affect teaching and learning in his school.

The Medical Research Council provided generous support for our work in the form of an MRC Studentship to Susie Mackenzie and an MRC project grant (No. G8410938N) to Charles Hulme. In addition, the Nuffield Foundation awarded a Social Science Research Fellowship to Charles Hulme for the academic year 1989-90. This award was an invaluable help in the finishing stages of writing this book. Thanks also go to North Yorkshire County Council Education Department for granting the second author time off from teaching duties to complete some of the experimental work reported here.

A number of other people deserve our thanks. Vicki Tordoff helped collect some of the data, and Andrew Monk gave generous advice on statistical issues. Two names will undoubtedly stand out for the number of times they are cited by us: Alan Baddeley and Graham Hitch. Both deserve an especially warm note of thanks. Alan provided the theoretical framework that has inspired this work, and has always been generous in sharing his knowledge of (and enthusiasm for!) working memory. It is also probably true to say that it is only as a result of reading Alan's first textbook on memory, that we came to do research on memory at all. Graham has also been a great help in discussing ideas about working memory with us and he also provided invaluable comments on a first draft of the entire manuscript. Susan Gathercole was also kind enough to offer her comments on an earlier version of the book. Maggie Snowling provided much needed help and encouragement in the later stages of writing. Her perceptive comments were particularly crucial in helping to sharpen the last two chapters. We should also like to thank Dave Gregory and the late Stephen Mackenzie for their help and support. We must reluctantly admit, however, after all this expert help, that any remaining errors are entirely our own fault.

CHAPTER 1

Severe Learning Difficulties: History, Definitions, and Terminology

People differ in how clever they are. Some people can learn a wide range of complex skills with ease, while others find learning even comparatively simple skills very difficult. When someone has learning difficulties of a general nature they may be described as mentally handicapped. In the past, a variety of terms that we would now consider offensive have been used to describe individuals with learning difficulties, such as natural fools, idiots, morons, slow-witted or feeble-minded. Whatever term is used it is generally agreed that mental handicap affects the individual's capacity to learn. Mental handicap results in people having incomplete, or arrested development of intellectual capacities. People with severe learning difficulties are most commonly described in terms of a lack of general intelligence or mental capacity, and a resulting impairment of mental development and learning.

IQ tests are central to our current definitions of learning difficulties. These tests, which derive directly from the pioneering work of Binet and Simon (1916) at the turn of the century, sample a range of skills, such as memory processes, knowledge of vocabulary, construction of visuo-spatial puzzles, verbal reasoning, and conceptual knowledge. The tests are standardized, by testing large and representative samples of people of different ages, to obtain norms for performance.

Standardization results in the tests having an average score of 100. The tests have also been developed to have normally distributed scores with a standard deviation of 15 points. Well-standardized tests should also be free from any sex bias. In spite of their statistical sophistication IQ tests are often heavily criticized. A common criticism has been the lack of any coherent underlying theory of what they measure. However, from a practical standpoint, they have proved extremely useful because they are simple to administer and correlate well with measures of scholastic achievement and other external criteria of learning ability.

Another measurement, related to IQ, that is often used to express the level of intellectual development is mental age (MA). Mental age is given simply by the level of attainment reached on a test in relation to the normal population. So, for example, if a child performs on an IQ test at a level equivalent to a 7-year-old they would be assigned a mental age of 7 years, even though their actual or chronological age might be substantially higher than this if they have learning difficulties.

The terminology used, and explanations given, as to why some individuals fail to develop normal learning abilities have changed over the centuries, reflecting changes in attitudes and increasing knowledge.

HISTORICAL BACKGROUND

Ann M. Clarke and A.D.B. Clarke (1974) mention historical documents from as early as the thirteenth century which make distinctions between a "born fool" and a "lunatic". If a man was classed a lunatic the Crown took possession of his land for the duration of his illness. However, a man found to be an idiot forfeited his property to the Crown permanently, but the Crown had the duty to provide for him. The purpose of classification during that period was, therefore, administrative.

Superstition ruled during the Middle Ages and there were commonly held beliefs that the "natural fool" (or his mother in pregnancy) had somehow been interfered with by fairies, witches or the devil. For example, the stories of "changelings", where the newly born child was said to be spirited away and replaced by another, may well have been used to explain why some people looked and acted differently from others.

A treatise by Paracelsus (published 1567) on the *Begetting of Idiots* is a colourful example of an early attempt to understand the nature of learning difficulties.

"It is astonishing that God, who redeemed man through the great price of His death and blood, lets men be born unwise

... that a thing is inborn is difficult; for what birth gives, who can take it away or remove it?
... as there is no disease, they are incurable [we] have no stones nor herbs whereby they might become intelligent."

Paracelsus (1567),
translated into English by Cranefield and Federn (1967).

The problem for Paracelsus lies in understanding why God allows some men to be born in a less than perfect state, especially when fools are born to normal parents. His explanation considers fools the fault of inexperienced craftsmen in God's "workshop". Parents provide the basic materials and God's craftsmen form the individual. Fools are produced not by the poor material provided by parents, but by the inexperienced apprentices who make mistakes and carve badly! (Cranefield & Federn, 1967).

The term "idiot" and the distinction of learning difficulties from insanity and lunacy were also well known in the seventeenth and eighteenth centuries. The following quotations show that their understanding of the nature of learning difficulties was not so very different from current views.

Madmen put wrong ideas together, and so make wrong propositions, but argue and reason right from them; but idiots make very few or no propositions, and reason scarce at all. John Locke (1623–1704).

... idiocy is not a disease, but a condition in which the intellectual faculties are never manifested; or have never been developed sufficiently to enable the idiot to acquire such an amount of knowledge as persons of his own age, and placed in similar circumstances as himself, are capable of receiving. Esquirol (1772–1840).

The nineteenth century brought certain changes. A growing medical interest in learning difficulties brought awareness of different degrees of "idiocy" and—by Itard and Seguin—the first systematic attempts at education or training for the subnormal. An "idiot" was now distinguished from an "imbecile", a "moron" or the "feeble-minded"; the feeble-minded being closest to normal, and idiots the very bottom of the range. These terms appear vague and confusing to us (is an idiot less intelligent than an imbecile, or vice versa?), but they were then the accepted scientific terms for differentiating the "mentally deficient". Translated into current IQ terms the feeble-minded and morons would be around 75 to 50 IQ points, imbeciles 50 to 20 IQ points, and idiots below 20 IQ points.

Our current definitions of learning difficulties centre on the use of IQ tests. The use of IQ tests as a means of defining mental handicap was formalized by a report of the World Health Organization. This used the term "mental subnormality" (World Health Organization, 1954); an individual was defined as mentally subnormal if their score was more than two standard deviations below the mean on an IQ test (i.e. an IQ of less than 70).

Distinctions about degrees of intellectual impairment have also been related to types of educational provision. Before 1971, many mentally handicapped children were considered ineducable and attended Junior Training Centres rather than schools. In the Education Act of 1971 a distinction was made between Educationally Subnormal (ESN) mild and severe. Generally, children with IQs in the 50 to 75 point range would attend an ESN (M) school, whereas children with a lower IQ would attend an ESN (S) school (the old Junior Training Centres). The equivalent American terminology was to speak of Educable Mental Retardates and Trainable Mental Retardates. There is no longer a distinction made between educable and ineducable children (Segal, 1967). All children with a mental handicap or subnormality, including the profoundly handicapped, now receive education adapted to their individual needs or "learning difficulties". These schools have been "redefined" in accord with the recommendations of the Warnock Report (1978) and are now referred to as "schools for children with moderate learning difficulties" and "schools for children with severe learning difficulties".

To summarize modern terminology: "mental subnormality" is a general term for all individuals with IQs of less than 70 points, "severe subnormality" (SSN) referring to those with an IQ of 50 to 20 points; "mental handicap" refers to a specific pathology which is known to affect mental development (and therefore results in a low IQ); "severe learning difficulty" (SLD) describes the effect of having a mental handicap or being severely subnormal, and has replaced the term "severely educationally subnormal" (ESN S); those with less severe impairments are said to have "moderate learning difficulties" (ESN M). To talk of learning difficulties is thought to be less pejorative than subnormality. In this text we will follow current terminology and use the term "learning difficulties" rather than "subnormality", even when describing research that used the older terminology. Finally, for reasons of clarity, the term "learning difficulties" should be distinguished from another term in wide current usage—"specific learning difficulties". This is a term used to refer to children who are experiencing difficulties with basic school subjects in the absence of any general learning difficulties, i.e. in children of average or near average IQ. Probably the most common problem of this sort is in children who have specific difficulties in learning to read and spell; this is sometimes referred to as developmental dyslexia.

THE INCIDENCE OF LEARNING DIFFICULTIES

People with learning difficulties are found in all areas of the world and in all social groups. It is difficult to calculate prevalence as this depends on individuals being diagnosed or identified administratively (Tizard, 1964). With school-age groups it is comparatively easy to make accurate estimates, as children with learning difficulties are often referred to outside agencies, such as psychologists, social services or child guidance centres. In older age groups many individuals with mild or moderate learning difficulties cope with life independently and will no longer be included in statistics. Most estimates cite 2% of the population, which in Britain is approximately one million individuals. In terms of educational provision, in 1967 there were 47,000 places available in schools for the "educationally subnormal" accounting for nearly 1% of the entire school population (A. D. B. Clarke & Ann. M. Clarke, 1975).

THE CAUSES OF LEARNING DIFFICULTIES

In general terms, the causes of learning difficulties can be divided into three broad categories: congenital, environmental, and pathological. In fact, for a large number of individuals there is no single identifiable cause; in practice, a number of factors will interact to affect mental development.

Genetic and Environmental Variation

Because of genetic differences amongst people and variations in the environments in which they develop, mental abilities show a wide dispersion when measured in large groups. The complex interaction between the many environmental and genetic factors that affect the development of intellectual differences amongst people results in mental ability, as assessed by IQ tests, having a normal distribution. This means that there will always be a small proportion of the population of superior ability with very much above average IQ. Conversely, there will always be a small proportion of people of inferior ability with IQs very much below the population average. It is assumed that most cases of mild learning difficulties result from an interaction of normal genetic and environmental variation; that is, from an inherited predisposition to develop a low IQ, in interaction with a range of adverse environmental factors, such as poor nutrition, health care, and educational opportunity.

Congenital Abnormalities

In addition to normal variations in genetic make-up that affect intellectual development, there are a variety of congenital pathological conditions that result in impairments of intellectual development. Some of these conditions are, fortunately, very rare, and it is not possible to give a full review of them here (Berg, 1974 and Milunsky, 1979 give comprehensive reviews of the clinical causes of retardation). The more common congenital disorders that result in mental handicap include metabolic disorders (such as phenylketonuria—PKU—gargoylism, and cretinism) and chromosome disorders, such as Down's syndrome (trisomy 21) and other rarer trisomies (Edward's syndrome, trisomy 18, and Patau's syndrome, trisomy 13).

Brain Damage

Damage to the brain early in life is a common cause of learning difficulties. Such damage may occur for a variety of reasons and at a variety of stages of development.

Prenatal maternal infections, such as rubella and syphilis, can adversely affect the brain of the developing foetus. Similarly, malnutrition or drugs taken during pregnancy can disturb foetal brain development, as may irradiation, or the mother's own antibodies, as in the case of rhesus incompatibility. Any of a wide range of factors that adversely affect the foetus prior to birth may result in impairments of brain function which later in life lead to learning difficulties.

Injury at birth may also result in brain damage and so to learning difficulties. Most commonly this may result from anoxia or hypoxia: too little or too much oxygen reaching the brain (Towbin, 1970). There may also be a raised incidence of reported obstetric complications, such as prolonged labour and forceps deliveries, amongst individuals who are later found to develop learning difficulties. It has been argued, however, that cause and effect may be difficult to untangle in such cases. At least in some cases, it has been argued, congenital abnormalities already present in the foetus may lead to obstetric problems and subsequent learning difficulties (Drillien, 1963). After birth there are rare cases where normal development is arrested or delayed as a result of an accident involving head injury, or because of infections that affect the central nervous system (such as meningitis, or whooping cough).

Interactions Between Congenital and Environmental Factors

It is important to emphasize, in the context of this brief discussion of pathological conditions that result in learning difficulties, that such conditions do not mean that development is fixed. Development in any individual will depend upon a complex interaction between inherited predispositions and environmental conditions. So, even in cases of severe learning difficulties that depend upon some clear pathology, the quality and quantity of environmental stimulation will almost certainly affect development. It is quite wrong to believe that a pathological condition results in some clear fixed limit to development.

One of the main types of study that has been used to demonstrate this has been to compare the development of children with severe learning difficulties living in different environments. A number of studies have compared the intellectual and social development of Down's syndrome children with severe learning difficulties, cared for at home rather than in institutions. There is evidence for better outcomes for such children when they are cared for at home (for reviews of these studies see Carr, 1985, and Gibson, 1978). There is some controversy over the interpretation of these studies, particularly as it is difficult to ensure comparability between groups before their placement in different settings. Gibson (1978) argued that many positive results in such studies may be artefacts of selective placement, whereby more severely handicapped children were more likely to be institutionalized. If this were true, it would be impossible to be sure whether differences in outcomes were really due to differences in the environmental stimulation that the children had received. However, as Carr (1985) points out, the consistency of the superiority of outcomes for home reared, as compared to institutionalized, Down's syndrome children is striking, and in some studies there is evidence for equivalent status between the groups compared at initial placement. Furthermore, in some studies institutionalization occurred at a very early age, before selective placement could operate on any sound basis. It seems reasonable to conclude, perhaps unsurprisingly, that environmental stimulation has beneficial effects on the development of Down's syndrome children, just as it does for normal children.

We may reflect on how fortunate it is that one of the practical aims of this research (to assess the advisability of placing children in institutions) has now become redundant. Current social policy has moved away from the idea of institutionalizing children whether they suffer from Down's syndrome or other forms of handicap. Theoretically, however, these studies provide important evidence for the plasticity of development in Down's syndrome and the potential for environmental influences on development. The range and magnitude of such influences, and whether they differ between normal and handicapped children are complex issues that are as yet far from resolved.

More recent studies of the effects of environmental stimulation on the development of Down's syndrome children have focused on the effects of early intervention programmes to provide added stimulation for the children. For example, Ludlow and Allen (1979) compared the development of two groups of Down's syndrome babies. The mothers of one group, from a single geographical area, attended a clinic twice a week with their children aged between 2 and 8 years. The children participated in nursery type activities and the mothers were encouraged to continue this stimulation at home. The control group from another area did not receive this extra stimulation. The results showed that the stimulated group were consistently ahead of the control group on standard measures of intellectual development (the Griffiths and Stanford-Binet scales), although both groups showed equivalent (and marked) intellectual decline as they got older. Cunningham (1982) also found that Down's syndrome infants, whose parents were given advice on ways of stimulating their babies, showed improvements. Babies for whom intervention started early showed least decline with increasing age in this study.

This brief discussion of the interaction between innate and environmental influences on development has implications for the interpretation of studies presented in later chapters. When differences in memory performance are documented between normal children and those with severe learning difficulties, it should not be assumed that such differences are in any way immutable. Being realistic, intellectual differences between normal children and those with severe learning difficulties may certainly be resistant to change but we do not yet know what critical environmental factors may impinge upon the development of intellectual skills, nor what the limits for change are.

INCIDENCE RATES FOR DIFFERENT FORMS OF PATHOLOGY IN SEVERE LEARNING DIFFICULTIES

This book will be concerned with severe learning difficulties, or, in IQ terms, with individuals whose IQs fall between 50 and 20 points. In terms of the different causes for their difficulties, the majority of individuals with IQs as low as this will have some recognized pathology.

Figures from the Centre for Child Study, Birmingham for the populations of schools for children with severe learning difficulties estimate that about 30% may have no diagnosed pathology (Smith & Phillips, 1981). A further 30% have Down's syndrome, and 30% will have other medical diagnoses, for instance, cerebral palsy, maternal rubella, and a variety of rarer chromosomal and genetic disorders. The remaining 10% of children in this range of subnormality will have shown normal development, for at least a number of months or possibly as much as two to three years, followed by a change in development. In about half of these cases this change will be due to a specific infection, head injury or poisoning causing damage to the central nervous system, for the rest there is no diagnosed cause.

The majority of individuals with severe learning difficulties therefore do have a diagnosed condition which accounts for their abnormal development. The figures from the Birmingham study suggest that 70% of this population have a recognized pathology; this includes about one-third with Down's syndrome (the most common chromosomal abnormality in man). Down's syndrome individuals are without doubt the largest single group in the population of those with severe learning difficulties, and because they form a large and homogeneous group there is a considerable body of scientific studies and knowledge about them. Of particular interest are their specific abnormalities of physical and central nervous system development and how these relate to their psychological development.

DOWN'S SYNDROME

Down's syndrome was first described as a specific condition by Langdon Down, an Edinburgh physician, in 1867. It was Down who noted the physical features typical of the syndrome and their similarity to the Asian race of mongols, and because of this the condition became known as mongolism. However individuals with the syndrome are found in all races of the world, and almost certainly existed long before Down's description of it. For instance, a late fifteenth-century Italian court painting of a Madonna and child shows an infant with all the physical signs of Down's syndrome (Stratford, 1982). High infant mortality rates and younger maternal age would lead one to expect fewer Down's syndrome births and very few Down's infants surviving the first 5 years of life in earlier times (Richards, 1968).

A major breakthrough in our understanding of the condition came in 1959, when it was discovered that the cells of people with Down's syndrome had 47 chromosomes, whereas a normal human has 46 (Lejeune, Gautier, & Turpin, 1959). The extra chromosome appears in pair 21, making it a trisomy (group of three). A small minority of Down's syndrome cases (approximately 5–6%) do not have an extra chromosome, but the trisomy in pair 21 is caused by the displacement of a chromosome from another pair, known as a translocation (Scully, 1973). Translocation is inherited directly from a normal parent who is a carrier with a "balanced translocation". In such cases there is high risk of Down's syndrome in siblings and in successive generations, but not in the more common trisomy pattern. Nevertheless, the abnormality is always related to the chromosome pair 21. In a small proportion of cases (2–3%) the trisomy is not present in all the body cells, but only in a proportion of them (there are a variety of forms); this is known as mosaicism (Gibson, 1978).

The Down's chromosome anomaly results in a deceleration of all aspects of development. This includes the development of the nervous system, which clearly has an effect on intellectual development. The new-born Down's syndrome infant is typically small, placid, and floppy due to hypotonia (lack of muscle tone). The central nervous system is immature and may have developed only to the level of a normal 6 to 7 month foetus: The brain is small and myelination is incomplete. Myelination is known to speed up neural transmission, therefore incomplete myelination may mean slower neural transmission in Down's syndrome.

The slowed rate of development observed in the Down's syndrome foetus persists as the child grows older. This slowed rate of development has consequences for the assessment of intellectual development in Down's syndrome using IQ tests and some other measures. IQ tests work by relating the performance of an individual to the average performance of a group of the same age. In Down's syndrome the delayed rate of development means that an increasing lag is observed between them and normal children as they mature. This has the effect that IQ in Down's syndrome is seen to fall from early childhood to adolescence. This does not mean that their performance on the test items gets worse as they get older, but simply that the difference between their performance and that of normal children increases, so that they fall further and further behind. We will discuss a similar pattern in relation to the failure of the development of short-term memory in Chapter 4.

There has been debate about whether the physical features and mental development of individuals with the rarer translocation and mosaicism patterns of Down's syndrome are the same as in the common trisomy 21 cases. There is some evidence (Gibson, 1978) that the severity of physical stigmata and degree of learning difficulties are less marked in mosaic cases than in "normal" trisomy 21 Down's syndrome cases. For example, Fischler (1975) compared 15 mosaic cases with 15 age and sex matched standard trisomy cases, and found the mosaic cases to be of higher IQ. The comparison of groups of equivalent age is essential given evidence of slower intellectual development and hence declining IQ with age in Down's syndrome (Carr, 1985; Gibson, 1978).

The head, and brain, of a Down's syndrome person is smaller than normal, and a different shape. Autopsy reports show that brain weight is considerably less than usual, a Down's adult might have a brain weight of 1,000 to 1,100 grams, approximately 90–70 % of normal brain weight (Benda, 1969). However, the cerebellum and brain stem are disproportionately small, being only 80–50 % of normal weight (Crome, Cowie, & Slater, 1966). This relates to the shape of the head in Down's syndrome: The length of the head is shorter than normal, but the width is normal.

As emphasized earlier, development, even in the presence of some clearly diagnosed pathology, will depend upon a complex interaction between inherited predispositions and environmental influences. This is as true in Down's syndrome as in any other developmental disorder. The Down's syndrome individual invariably suffers some degree of learning difficulty but, as in normal children, ability varies considerably (LaVeck & Brehm, 1978). It is important to emphasize that environmental factors will affect mental development in Down's syndrome, just as it does in normal children.

The potential achievement of people with Down's syndrome, as with other people with learning difficulties, is constantly being reviewed as education and care improve. At the beginning of this century the Down's syndrome adult was considered equal to a 5-year-old child (Goddard, 1916; Brousseau, 1928). More contemporary authors put the upper limit of mental ability for Down's adults at mental age 7 to 8 years (Nakamura, 1961; Gibson, 1978). As medical and educational provision improves, it will be interesting to see what mental achievements are made by later generations of Down's syndrome people.

DIFFERENCES BETWEEN DOWN'S SYNDROME AND OTHER FORMS OF SEVERE LEARNING DIFFICULTIES

Down's syndrome is the most common cause of severe learning difficulties in developed countries, and is unique because it has a relatively well-understood biological basis that allows it to be identified early. For all these reasons there has been a great deal of interest in whether there are qualitative differences between Down's syndrome people and those with equally severe learning difficulties of other aetiologies. The strategy in such studies is to compare the performance of Down's syndrome subjects with other subjects with equally severe learning difficulties matched for mental age. That is, with a group of subjects with severe learning difficulties who have achieved the same absolute level of performance on a test of general ability. A number of cognitive skills have been examined in such studies. Here, we can do no more than summarize some of the major findings.

Motor Problems

Langdon Down (1867) himself noted that motor inco-ordination was common in "mongols". Many more recent studies have confirmed and expanded upon this observation (for reviews, see Anwar, 1981a; Henderson, 1985). Carr (1975) studied a group of Down's babies and a group of normal babies longitudinally in their first four years of life. She found deficits in motor ability in the Down's babies (assessed using the Bayley Scales) and the difference between the Down's babies and the controls increased with increasing age. At the age of 4 years the Down's children had motor skills typical of a normal 2-year-old child. This study, like others mentioned earlier, documents the slower rate of development in Down's, compared to normal children, which results in increasingly severe deficits with increasing age.

One source of the motor difficulties in Down's syndrome appears to be a deficiency in the ability to set up motor programmes to guide movements. U. Frith and C. D. Frith (1974) compared groups of Down's syndrome, normal, autistic, and other children with severe learning difficulties matched for mental age, on a rotary pursuit tracking task (moving a stylus to follow a moving spot of light). Improvements on this task over trials were taken as evidence for learning motor programmes (stored repetitive sequences of movements). The Down's syndrome children showed less improvement across trials than did the other three groups, indicating a selective deficit in the learning of motor programmes. These difficulties in learning motor programmes in Down's syndrome children may well be relevant to experiments reported later in this book concerned with the use of articulatory coding in short-term memory tasks. The speech difficulties in Down's syndrome children, which are related to their short-term memory difficulties, may well be caused by their difficulties in the motor control of speaking.

These difficulties in developing motor programmes may in turn depend on perceptual difficulties. Anwar (1981b) found evidence for Down's subjects having more difficulty in using visual and kinaesthetic feedback (information about the position of their limbs and their relationship to objects in the environment), to control movements than mental age-matched normal subjects and other subjects with severe learning difficulties. Clearly such difficulties might lead to problems in making appropriate movements, and in turn lead to deficits in the creation of motor programmes of the sort seen in the syndrome.

Language Development

Late onset of language and slow, somewhat slurred, speech are typical of Down's syndrome (Down & Langdon, 1867; Benda, 1969; Gibson, 1978). Dodd (1972) found similar patterns of babbling in Down's syndrome and normal infants. It has been speculated that the slow transition from babbling to speaking in Down's syndrome may relate to the complexity of the motor requirements of learning to talk.

Down's syndrome is also characterized by structural abnormalities of the mouth and vocal tract. The mouth is smaller than usual, restricting movement of the tongue, which may help to explain the articulation problems that are typical of the syndrome (Schlanger & Gottsleben, 1957; Dodd, 1976). These structural abnormalities are likely to add to difficulties with articulation due to motor programming deficits in Down's syndrome. It is not, of course, possible to rule out more central difficulties contributing to the speech difficulties in Down's syndrome, but it has often been noted that expressive language functions are consistently below the levels of receptive skills in the syndrome (Benda, 1969; Gibson, 1978)

COGNITIVE PROBLEMS ASSOCIATED WITH LOW IQ

People with learning difficulties are, by definition, slow in learning skills and abilities in relation to the normal population. There are particular areas of psychological development in which problems are common amongst those with severe learning difficulties. Since the 1960s there has been growing research interest in the specific skills and cognitive processes that cause these individuals particular difficulty.

People with learning difficulties obey the same laws of development and learning as do normal individuals, in terms of Piagetian stages of development (Woodward, 1979), or learning theory (Carr, 1980; Zeaman & House, 1963) and in their acquisition of language (Lenneberg, 1967). Although there has been a great deal of debate as to whether the development of those with severe learning difficulties is best characterized as delayed or deviant, there is to date no good evidence for qualitative differences in psychological processes.

Another area showing quantitative impairments in those with severe learning difficulties is in the speed of information processing. As IQ falls the processing of information becomes slower, as shown by slower reaction times (Berkson, 1960; Jensen, 1981; Weaver & Ravaris, 1970).

It is also noticeable that problems with language increase as IQ falls, especially in relation to language production rather than comprehension (Mittler, 1974; Schlanger & Gottsleben, 1957; Spreen, 1965). There is also evidence of attentional problems in people with learning difficulties. There is the difficulty in attending to the relevant aspect of a discrimination (Zeaman & House, 1963, 1979), a shorter span of attention (time spent concentrating on one object or task), and greater distractibility than in normal subjects (Boersma & Muir, 1975).

There has been considerable research on memory processes in people with learning difficulties; memory is clearly an important part of learning processes. Generally, people with learning difficulties are described as having short-term memory problems rather than long-term memory problems (Ann M. Clarke & A. D. B. Clarke, 1974; N.R. Ellis, 1978). Belmont (1966), reviewing a number of studies of long-term memory, concluded that although initial learning, or acquisition, is poor in those with learning difficulties compared to normal subjects, rate of forgetting over long periods is the same. However, Elliot (1978) found slower retrieval of information from long-term memory in people with severe learning difficulties. People with severe learning difficulties are described as having a more limited long-term database, as their acquisition of information is at a lower level than normal (Belmont, 1966). Their short-term memory problems have also been a source of much research, and this will be discussed in detail in the next chapter.

A FEW WORDS ABOUT METHODOLOGY

In studying memory or any other cognitive process in children with severe learning difficulties a number of methodological issues arise. These issues are common in other areas of developmental psychology, but they may be relatively unfamiliar to readers whose prime interest is in memory processes.

The first consists of the choice of control group. Two different control groups are common, a group of children of the same chronological age (a CA match) or a group of children of the same mental age (an MA match). Because, by definition, children with severe learning difficulties show massive impairments on most intellectual tasks, differences between them and CA matched groups are virtually guaranteed. Such differences are relatively uninformative.

Matching for MA is a better design. Here, by selecting younger normal children, we can show that the two groups being compared have reached an equivalent level of intellectual development on standardized test. If we then find that the group with learning difficulties have lower scores than the MA controls, we have evidence for them having some special difficulty on the task in question. Findings in a simple one-condition experiment with such a design are fraught with difficulties, however, because there are clearly dangers that any putative deficit (in memory, for example) may be a non-specific consequence of some other difficulty (problems of attention, or understanding experimental instructions). A more convincing strategy is to compare two or more conditions, and look for interactions between groups and conditions. Such interactions may then provide evidence for a differential deficit in children with severe learning difficulties. This is the approach that will be used in some later chapters of this book.

Another issue concerns the use of cross-sectional and longitudinal designs in the search for patterns of developmental change. In cross-sectional studies groups are selected at different stages of development (CA or MA). If younger groups show different patterns of performance than older groups, this is suggestive of a developmental change in the pattern of performance. However, strictly, inferences about developmental changes cannot be made from cross-sectional studies alone. If we wish to find evidence for changes in certain processes as a result of development, a more certain path is provided by longitudinal studies where the same individuals are tested on a number of different occasions. This is the approach that has been used in a number of studies of the development of Down's syndrome described earlier, which have shown differences in the rate of cognitive development between Down's syndrome and normal children. We will use a combination of cross-sectional and longitudinal studies to infer developmental changes in memory processes in studies reported in later chapters.

CHAPTER 2

Working Memory:
Structure and Function

MEMORY SPAN

Memory span is the most commonly used measure of short-term memory and refers to the number of words a person can recall in order immediately after hearing them. The study of memory span has a long history in experimental psychology. As early as 1885 Ebbinghaus noted that he could recite a list of up to seven unrelated words at the first attempt, but longer lists took more trials; the longer the list, the greater the number of trials before he could recall it correctly. Jacobs (1887) was the first psychologist to have used a standard memory span test with a wide range of individuals. Jacobs gave individuals a series of lists of increasing length to determine memory span, defined as the longest list that could be recalled in correct order. He made three main observations, which still stand today: memory span varies according to the material used; span is less in children than it is in adults; span varies according to "natural ability" (intelligence).

It was soon established that memory span shows a gradual increase with age. Memory span was also quickly accepted as a useful index of mental capacity. A memory span test (using sequences of digits of increasing length) was included in the first test of mental development devised by Binet and Simon, and a digit span test is still a part of modern IQ and mental ability tests, such as the Wechsler Intelligence Scale for Children (WISC), the British Ability Scales (BAS), and the Illinois Test of Psycholinguistic Abilities (ITPA). Digit span is included in such tests because there is a gradual, steady increase in performance on the test from the age of 4 to 5 years to around 16 years. At age 4 the individual can recall on average just 3 digits in order, but performance normally improves steadily to about 6 digits at age 10 or 12; then there is a more gentle increase up to age 16 when digit span plateaus at around 7 to 8 items.

When the Wechsler Intelligence Scale for Children was revised in 1976 the digit span sub-test was found to correlate moderately with the full-score IQ based on 10 sub-tests ($r = 0.43$). Not surprisingly, the correlation of digit span with the other five language sub-tests ($r = 0.45$) was higher than with the six performance tests ($r = 0.34$). These figures are based on the performance of 1,100 normal children aged 6 to 16 used in the standardization and revision of the WISC (Wechsler, 1976). Bachelder and Denny (1977) reviewed a number of studies in which a wider IQ range was included (normal children and those with learning difficulties). They found that when a broader IQ range is sampled, the correlation coefficient between digit span and other IQ sub-tests increases to figures in the 0.6 to 0.8 range.

Just as the increase in memory span is a consistent feature of normal development, so it has often been noted that memory span is impaired in groups with learning difficulties. In the 1880s, Galton measured memory span in "feeble-minded" individuals (i.e. those with learning difficulties), and found that although span varied amongst those classed as feeble-minded, their memory span was lower than that of normal individuals. More recent studies have shown that digit span is poor in those with learning difficulties, even in relation to many other tests of ability (Baumeister & Bartlett, 1962; Belmont, Birch, & Belmont, 1967; Marinosson, 1974).

These apparently stable relationships between memory span and age, and memory span and IQ, have been known and accepted for nearly a century. We must now consider the nature, and importance, of these relationships. One possible explanation draws on the idea that span reflects some general limitation on the human information processing system. Before considering this idea in more detail we will first consider, from an historical perspective, theories of short-term memory.

LIMITED CAPACITY TEMPORARY STORES

During the 1960s and 1970s there were numerous attempts to produce a model of the human memory system. An edited volume published in 1970 included more than 10 different models of human memory (Norman, 1970). Many of the models conceived memory as consisting of a number of stores distinguished by the time for which they held information (this became known as the "modal" model). These "multistore" models of memory consider that different forms of analysis and storage take place in different parts of the memory system. The most influential of these models was that of Atkinson and Shiffrin (1968), based on Broadbent (1958). This approach divided memory into three major types of store: a sensory store; a short-term store (STS); and a long-term store (LTS).

This division of memory into short- and long-term components proved very useful as a framework for experimental research. In time, however, a number of problems associated with the modal model emerged. For instance, the relationship between the long- and short-term stores and the question of whether information has to pass through short-term memory in order to reach the long-term store. However, this model remains a very popular framework within which to interpret adult memory performance, as well as that of normal children and those with learning difficulties.

The short-term memory store, as outlined by Atkinson and Shiffrin (1968), holds information in a verbal form and relies on the process of rehearsal (sub-vocal repetition) to maintain information in the store. Material held in the short-term store fades, or decays, if not maintained by rehearsal (J. Brown, 1958; L. R. Peterson & M. J. Peterson, 1959). Another cause of forgetting in such a system is displacement: Because the store has a limited capacity, old items have to make way for new. These notions were consistent with performance on many tests of short-term retention, including the memory span test, which show that an individual can take in and recall only a limited amount of information at any one time. Although short-term memory performance can be improved by the use of organizing strategies, it cannot be extended beyond the limits of the system (Craik, 1970). This contrasts with the apparently limitless capacity of the long-term store, and the permanence of its contents.

An important distinction needs to be made between the concept of a short-term memory system or short-term store and a short-term memory test such as the immediate serial recall of a list of items. Performance on a short-term memory test will depend on the information processing system as a whole, and in particular there is evidence that performance in immediate serial recall tasks involves output from both long- and short-term components (Waugh & Norman, 1965). Performance on a short-term memory test (such as the number of words recalled in a memory span test) does not reflect simply the contents of the short-term store.

The nature of the limit to the capacity of the short-term store has been the subject of a great deal of research. Broadbent (1958) suggested that as material decays in the short-term store, capacity might depend on how fast the individual could re-activate items. Waugh and Norman (1965) put forward an alternative view; that the short-term store consisted of a fixed number of "slots" or spaces, with capacity depending on how much the individual could put in each slot.

The concept of slots, or the pigeon hole theory, was related to information theory and capacity defined in terms of "bits" or "chunks". If the short-term store is limited by the number of bits of information stored, we should be able to remember long strings of binary digits, a few letters or digits, and very few words. This is not the case, Miller (1956) found that immediate memory for letters and digits was similar to that for words; about seven items in each case. Miller concluded that the capacity of immediate memory (short-term memory rather than the short-term store) was about seven chunks, or meaningful units of information.

Unfortunately for the chunk view, memory span for different types of material does vary, with memory span for some types of material being considerably better than that for others. The clearest demonstration of this was provided by Baddeley, Thomson, & Buchanan (1975). They looked at serial recall of words of one to five syllables and found that recall of short (one syllable) words was much better than recall of long words (five syllables). This result clearly cannot be explained in terms of slots as each word would represent one chunk, or slot. In the chunk view of short-term memory capacity, serial recall for long words should be the same as that for short words. Baddeley et al. showed that the time taken to articulate the words used in a short-term memory task was crucial. This relationship between memory span and articulation rate is discussed in detail in the next section.

The concept of a limited capacity temporary store has been a very useful one, both in interpreting the results of experiments and also in understanding everyday memory problems. Much research in the past 20 years (on adults, children, and those with learning difficulties) has been based on a general framework that distinguishes short- from long-term memory stores. There are, however, problems connected with this view, such as the nature of the short-term store and the relationship between the long- and short-term systems (for instance whether information has to pass through short-term memory to reach, or be retrieved from, the long-term store). A more detailed description of short-term memory was outlined by Baddeley and Hitch (1974) and recently revised by Baddeley (1986); this is known as the working memory approach.

WORKING MEMORY

Some of the evident problems with the modal model of memory influenced Baddeley and Hitch's attempt to formulate an alternative framework for research on short-term memory. This work brought to prominence the term "working memory".

Working memory is a term, like some others in psychology, that suffers because different people use it in subtly different ways. In its broadest sense, working memory refers to the use of temporary storage mechanisms in the performance of more complex tasks. So, for example, in order to read and understand prose, we must be able to hold incoming information in memory. This is necessary in order to compute the semantic and syntactic relationships among successive words, phrases, and sentences and so construct a coherent and meaningful re-presentation of the meaning of the text. This temporary storage of information during reading is said to depend on working memory. In this view the ability to understand prose will depend on, among other things, the capacity of a person's working memory system. Such temporary storage of information is obviously necessary for the performance of a wide variety of other tasks apart from reading, such as mental arithmetic (Hitch, 1978) and verbal reasoning (Baddeley & Hitch, 1974). This definition of working memory then, is a functional term. Working memory is the system (or more accurately the set of systems) responsible for the temporary storage of information during the performance of cognitive tasks.

It is no coincidence that the examples just mentioned, of the functional importance of the temporary storage of information in working memory, involve verbal material where it is relatively easy to think of culturally important skills. It is almost certainly true, however, that equivalent systems exist for information coded in different forms. So, in the visual modality, the temporary storage of information is likely to be important in solving visuo-spatial problems and may limit the development of mechanical, drawing, and design skills. But this at the moment remains speculative. We concentrate here on working memory for verbal materials but this does not imply that other forms of working memory are unimportant or uninteresting.

In contrast to this use of working memory as a functional term, a majority of terms in memory research are concerned with structural, rather than functional, distinctions. The best known examples of this sort are short- and long-term memory, which we have discussed earlier. These terms are used to refer to distinct hypothetical memory stores with different characteristics (in terms of coding, capacity, and so on). The term working memory has sometimes been seen as synonymous with the concept of short-term memory (e.g. Klatzky, 1975). We would argue that such a direct alignment leads to confusion. It may be accurate to argue that short-term memory functions as a working memory system in certain tasks so that the storage capacity of short-term memory is important for their performance (e.g. mental arithmetic). But that, of course, does not mean that other systems do not also contribute to such storage. This alignment between the concepts of short-term and working memory has probably been reinforced by the now classic working memory model of Baddeley and Hitch (1974; Baddeley, 1986). This model, which was motivated by a desire to relate short-term memory to the performance of more complex cognitive tasks is, we argue, best seen as a relatively explicit structural model of short-term memory processes. There may, however, be important aspects of working memory storage that are not captured by this model. In this view the importance of the concept of working memory, as a functional term (which seems central to so much work in cognitive psychology) needs to be distinguished from the adequacy of the Baddeley and Hitch model as a structural model, used to account for many short-term memory phenomena. Criticisms of the model, in relation to its explanatory adequacy as a structural model accounting for performance in short-term memory tasks, are relatively independent of issues concerned with the importance of the concept of working memory as a functional term.

We turn now to consider the structural properties of the Baddeley and Hitch model of working memory.

BADDELEY AND HITCH'S WORKING MEMORY MODEL

Resdearch generated by the modal model paid lip-service to the idea that short-term memory played a role as a working memory system in more complex tasks, such as reading and mental arithmetic. However, research within this framework concentrated very much on understanding the mechanisms underlying traditional short-term memory tasks, such as memory span, at the expense of trying, directly, to relate short-term memory to the performance of these more complex skills.

Baddeley and Hitch (1974) explicitly set out to redress this imbalance and, in the process, their classic work highlighted certain shortcomings of the modal model. This led them to propose a model of working memory which puts great emphasis on the functions of memory in the processing and flow of information in everyday activities, such as the need to retain and integrate information for short periods when reading. The main difference between the working memory model and previous concepts of short-term memory is that it is seen as a complex of stores and systems rather than as a unitary store (Baddeley, 1983, 1986; Baddeley & Hitch, 1974). Baddeley (1983, 1986) describes working memory as a limited capacity central executive interacting with a set of passive slave sub-systems. The basic structure of the model is outlined in Fig. 2.1.

Baddeley describes two particular slave sub-systems both used for temporary storage of different classes of information: the speech-based articulatory loop; and the visual image scratch-pad. As memory span is an auditory test, with verbal recall, it is the speech-based articulatory loop that is particularly relevant to memory span performance. The visual image scratch-pad is concerned, as its name suggests, with the maintenance of visuo-spatial information in short-term memory. As such it has little relevance to explanations of auditory verbal short-term memory, and will not be dealt with further here.

The central executive, described by Baddeley (1983, 1986), is of limited capacity and controls the manipulation and flow of information, while a small amount of information may be retained in slave stores, such as the articulatory loop. The importance of the articulatory loop is that once verbal information is placed in the loop it can be kept available

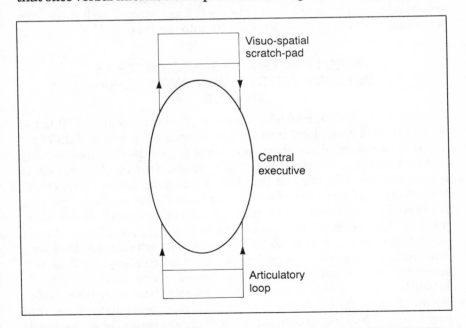

FIG. 2.1. A simplified representation of the working memory model. From Baddeley, A.D. (1990). Human Memory: Theory and Practice. Hove, U.K.: Lawrence Erlbaum Associates Ltd.

(using rehearsal) without taking up the processing capacity of the executive. The remaining capacity of the executive is therefore available for retrieving relevant information from other parts of the memory system, deciding what is or is not relevant, and forming associations and relationships between items.

THE ARTICULATORY LOOP

The limited capacity of the articulatory loop is defined in terms of time. A useful analogy is a tape loop of specific length which can hold a message which fits onto the length of the tape. The temporal duration of the message will determine whether it fits on the tape loop, if it is too long some of the message will be lost or have to be stored in the central executive. Assuming that tape speed is constant, if you have 15 minutes worth of tape you can fill it with one piece of music lasting 15 minutes, or three pieces of music each lasting five minutes, and so on. Following this analogy the number of items that can be fitted on the articulatory loop (words, digits, etc.) depends on the time taken to articulate them. The words are stored in the loop in a fixed temporal sequence and rehearsal amounts to re-identifying the fading traces of each successive word and re-writing it (re-recording it) onto the tape.

WORD LENGTH AND SPEECH RATE AS DETERMINANTS OF IMMEDIATE SERIAL RECALL

As mentioned earlier, Baddeley Thomson, and Buchanan (1975) found a difference in immediate memory (serial recall) for words of different lengths. Serial recall of short, one syllable, words was considerably better than that for long, five syllable, words. This word-length effect can be explained by the fact that long words take longer to articulate than short words and therefore take up more of the available space on the tape loop. The effect of articulation duration was clearly shown when memory for words of the same number of syllables, but different articulation times, was tested. One set of two syllable words of long duration (e.g. harpoon, Friday, cyclone: mean articulation time 0.8s) was compared with a set of two syllable words which took less time to articulate (e.g. wicket, pectin, bishop: mean articulation time 0.44s). Recall of words that took less time to say was better than for those that took longer. Thus, even when the number of syllables is the same, words with shorter articulation time are better recalled.

Further investigation of reading rates and recall for different words (one to five syllables) showed a consistent relationship between word length, recall, and reading rate. This relationship is shown in Fig. 2.2. As word length increases, memory span and reading rate both fall. Baddeley et al. showed that subjects could recall as many words as they could read in approximately 1.8 seconds. Thus, the capacity of the articulatory loop (which they estimated from the slope of the speech rate-recall function) can be best expressed, not as a number of items, but rather as the time taken to articulate a sequence of items. The linear relationship between reading rate and memory span, which is used to estimate the capacity of the rehearsal loop, is defined as follows:

$$\text{words held on loop} = \text{Length of loop} \times \text{speech rate}$$

$$\text{words} = T \text{ seconds} \times \text{words per second}$$

The length of the loop, T, is constant, let us say 1.5 seconds. Therefore for short words that can be spoken at a rate of four a second, six words can be held on the loop ($6 = 1.5 \times 4$). For long words which take twice as long to say (two words per second), half as many words can be held on the loop, three words = 1.5×2.

There is a great deal of evidence from other studies which supports the idea of an articulatory loop. Standing, Bond, Smith, and Isely (1980) found that memory span for eight different types of material was closely related to sub-vocalization rate (articulation time). This was true across both subjects and materials. People with slow sub-vocalization times had lower spans, and span was lower for materials that took longer to sub-vocalize. Testing bilingual subjects in their second language gave lower sub-vocalization rates and proportionally lower spans. Standing et al. showed that memory span was roughly constant in terms of the number of items that could be sub-vocalized in 1.8 to 2.2 seconds.

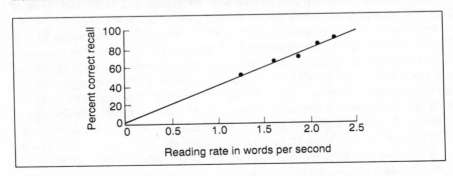

FIG. 2.2. The relationship between reading rate and recall. (From Baddeley et al., 1975.)

Schweickert and Boruff (1986) proposed a mathematical model of the articulatory loop. They measured memory span for a variety of materials and related span to the time taken to recite lists of span length. Span was roughly constant when expressed in terms of the time taken to recite a sequence; subjects recalled as many items as they could articulate in about 1.8 to 1.9 seconds. Wright (1979) has also argued convincingly that differences in articulation duration between high- and low-frequency words provides at least part of the explanation for the finding that high-frequency words are recalled better in serial recall tasks (Watkins, 1977, but see also Gregg, Freedman & Smith, (1989), and Hulme, Maughan, & Brown, (1991) for further discussion of the effects of word frequency on short-term memory).

Another type of evidence that supports the notion of the articulatory loop comes from comparisons of memory span across different languages. N. C. Ellis and Hennelly (1980) found that Welsh digits take longer to articulate than English digit names, and that in bilingual subjects span for digits spoken in English is longer than span for digits spoken in Welsh. This finding was extended by Naveh-Benjamin and Ayres (1986) who found a roughly linear relationship between articulation rate and digit span across four languages (English, Spanish, Hebrew, and Arabic). Estimates of memory span in these different languages showed that it was roughly constant as the number of items that could be said in 1.83 to 2.13 seconds. These figures accord very closely with the values obtained by Baddeley et al. (1975), Schweickert and Boruff (1986), and Standing et al. (1980)

A possible wrinkle on this extremely neat picture comes from some recent experiments concerned with memory for verbal materials in Chinese. Zhang and Simon (1985) report several experiments concerned with memory span for different forms of written Chinese materials. The early experiments in this series are all concerned with the ease of encoding materials into a speech-based code and are entirely consistent with the notion of an articulatory loop. The last two experiments Zhang and Simon report are concerned with memory for numbers and lead them to question the adequacy of the articulatory loop as a theory of immediate serial recall performance. In the first of these experiments, they compare memory span for spoken lists of Chinese and English digits in Chinese bilingual subjects. Digit span is substantially higher for the Chinese digits, which they attribute to their greater familiarity to their subjects. This, in turn, they speculate, may lead to differences in the rate at which the digit names are articulated. Although this may be the case, they ignore the possibility of structural differences between their stimuli leading to differences in articulation speed that are relatively independent of familiarity. The average span they quote, of

5.67 for English digits, is certainly low in comparison to reasonable estimates of digit span for English-speaking adults (about 7–8). However, in contrast, the average span obtained by their subjects for Chinese digits (9.5) is certainly much higher than this figure. This suggests that perhaps there are structural differences between the digit names in Chinese and English that lead them to be articulated more quickly, and so recalled better. Unfortunately, Zhang and Simon do not measure articulation rate for the materials in their experiment. In their last experiment they measure memory span for sequences of characters (symbols that have a one syllable pronunciation, but that do not normally occur in isolation), words and idioms (meaningful pairs of words). They find that span (in terms of syllables) is not constant across these materials, but increases from characters to words and from words to idioms. They go on to fit an equation to their data that predicts span from a composite of rehearsal rate and the number of chunks of which the sequence is composed. In their equation the number of chunks (meaningful units) recalled is a function of three parameters: T, the fixed temporal capacity of the articulatory loop; a, the amount of time it takes to bring each chunk into the articulatory mechanism and articulate its first syllable; and b, the time it takes to articulate each syllable in the chunk beyond the first one. Because Zhang and Simon never directly measure articulation rate for the materials used in their experiments it remains unclear, from their data, to what extent a separate role for the number of syllables memorized is necessary. Furthermore, using meaningful sequences of words (idioms) complicates the picture further, because such sequences of words may recruit the use of long-term memory to a greater degree than do meaningless sequences of unrelated words of the sort invariably used in studies of short-term memory.

Data from another experiment on Chinese subjects suggests that the results obtained by Zhang and Simon, may, after all, be consistent with a simpler view of the articulatory loop that excludes discussion of "chunks". Stigler, Lee, and Stevenson (1986) compared digit span in Chinese and English. Digit span was consistently higher in Chinese than in English subjects, both in children and in adults. More crucially, they also measured articulation rate for the digit names in their English and Chinese subjects, with a simple outcome: Differences in digit span between the two languages are perfectly well predicted by the faster rate of articulation for the Chinese digit names. This, therefore, emphasizes the criticism of Zhang and Simon's experiment, and shows that a separate role for the number of syllables memorized, over and above the overall rate of articulation of items, is probably not warranted.

To summarize these studies, serial recall performance, the basis of immediate memory span, is closely related to the time it takes to articulate the material to be recalled. Various studies using slightly different methodologies suggest that subjects can recall as much as they can say in roughly two seconds.

This consistent relationship between articulation rate and memory span provides clear support for the notion of an articulatory loop (Baddeley & Hitch, 1974). This store holds information in an articulatory form and is subject to the passive loss of information due to decay. However, rehearsal, consisting of the cyclic re-activation of speech motor programmes, can overcome this loss of information, providing the total duration of the sequence of items to be remembered does not exceed the decay time of the store (about two seconds). This view provides a particularly elegant explanation for the effects of word length on serial recall, which in turn can be used to explain variations in memory span between words of different frequency and also the variations in digit span observed across different languages. Furthermore, the relationship between articulation rate and memory span also provides an explanation for individual differences in memory span; individuals with high articulation rates also tend to have high memory spans and vice versa. None of this should be taken to suggest that the articulatory loop provides a sufficient explanation for all aspects of memory span performance. Some limitations on the explanation of serial recall performance purely in terms of the articulatory loop will be considered later.

The Acoustic Similarity Effect

The effect of word length on serial recall is one demonstration of the effect of speech coding in short-term memory. The other classic demonstration of this is the effect of acoustic similarity; people find it more difficult to remember lists of words or consonants which sound similar, even when they are presented visually (Baddeley, 1966; Conrad, 1964; Conrad & Hull, 1964). The effects of word length and acoustic similarity were both traditionally seen as attributable to the operation of the same speech-coded short-term memory system.

More recently, Baddeley has challenged this view. In the latest refinement of the working memory model, the articulatory loop is divided into two components: a phonological input store; and an articulatory rehearsal process (Baddeley, 1983, 1986; Salame & Baddeley, 1982). In this view, the effects of acoustic similarity are attributed to the laying down of similar, and so confusable, traces in the phonological input store. The effects of word length are again attributable to the articulatory rehearsal process. In order to understand the reasons for splitting the loop into two components, and possible objections to it, it is necessary to consider some other types of evidence.

THE EFFECTS OF ARTICULATORY SUPPRESSION

Articulatory suppression involves the subject having to intone some irrelevant words such as "the,the,the" while holding other words in short-term memory. This procedure is designed to make articulatory rehearsal difficult or impossible and, not surprisingly, it dramatically impairs short-term memory performance. More interestingly, however, it also has selective effects on recall of different types of material. In particular, the markers for speech-based coding, the word-length and acoustic similarity effects, are abolished by suppression when presentation of material is visual; with auditory presentation, although the word-length effect is abolished, the acoustic similarity effect remains, albeit in an attenuated form (Baddeley, Lewis, & Vallar, 1984).

These findings are interpreted thus: with visually presented material, articulatory suppression, by preventing articulation, blocks encoding into the loop. For visually presented material, sub-vocal speech appears to be necessary to encode material phonologically into the passive phonological store. Hence, the acoustic similarity effect and word-length effect are abolished by suppression when presentation is visual, because the material is simply never encoded into a speech-based form. For auditory inputs, on the other hand, speech gains obligatory access to the phonological input store. Thus, with auditory presentation, the acoustic similarity effect still occurs under conditions of articulatory suppression, because the information gains obligatory access to the input store, the locus of this effect. The word-length effect is abolished however, because it depends on the rehearsal of an articulatory code and this is prevented by suppression. Suppression, therefore, is seen to have a dual effect, it prevents encoding of visual material into a speech-based form, and for material so encoded, it prevents articulatory rehearsal.

In summary, the fact that the acoustic similarity effect survives articulatory suppression has been used to argue that the effect does not depend on rehearsal. Instead, it is argued, the occurrence of this effect depends on the occurrence of confusions within a passive phonological input store. The contents of this store can in turn be refreshed by articulatory rehearsal.

The Unattended Speech Effect

The other major piece of evidence that has led to the postulation of the two-component view of the articulatory loop is the unattended-speech effect (Salame & Baddeley, 1982); memory for visually presented words is impaired by the simultaneous presentation of spoken material, which the subject is told, quite explicitly, to ignore. This effect is specific to speech (noise has very little effect), and is greater when the unattended speech is phonologically similar to the material that is presented to be remembered. The unattended speech effect is seen as resulting from interference between the unattended speech and items that are being held in the phonological input store. The effects of unattended speech on recall are eliminated by articulatory suppression (how many things is it reasonable for people to do at one time?!). This is interpreted in terms of suppression preventing encoding into the passive input store, which it is argued is the locus of interference from unattended speech.

This effect of suppression on the unattended-speech effect has been studied further by Hanley and C. Broadbent (1987) who looked at the effects of unattended speech when the material to be remembered was presented auditorily. They found that unattended speech continued to have an effect on recall when subjects were suppressing. Here, they argued, the material is encoded obligatorily into the passive input store, where unattended speech then causes interference with recall.

OBJECTIONS TO A TWO-COMPONENT VIEW OF THE ARTICULATORY LOOP: IS A SEPARATE PHONOLOGICAL INPUT STORE NECESSARY?

Hulme (1986; Hulme & Tordoff, 1989) has argued that many of the effects used to support the idea of a separate phonological input store can be accommodated within a unitary view of the articulatory loop. We will consider these arguments now.

Hulme (1984) studied the effects of acoustic similarity on memory span in children ranging in age from 4 to 10 years. As expected, memory span showed large increases across this range of ages, but, more importantly, the difference in recall of acoustically similar and dissimilar lists also increased with increasing age. In 4-year-olds, span did not differ reliably for similar and dissimilar lists. The difference was reliable, however, in the 5-year-olds and this difference increased steadily between the ages of 5 and 10. The pattern of changes was such that increases in span with age for the dissimilar items was much more marked than for the similar items. It was argued that this pattern of results was plausibly related to changes in the efficiency or speed of rehearsal within the articulatory loop with age. If similarity between traces in the articulatory loop leads to confusions between items during

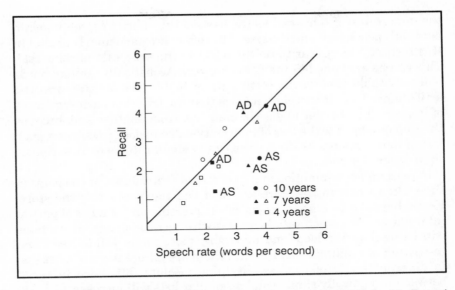

FIG. 2.3. Mean number of words recalled per list versus speech rate for 10-, 7-, and 4-year old children. Unfilled symbols denote data for words of different length; filled symbols denote data for acoustically similar (AS) and acoustically dissimilar (AD) words. (From Hulme & Tordoff, 1989).

rehearsal, then this should lead to more problems in recalling similar than dissimilar lists.

This idea was pursued further by Hulme and Tordoff (1989). In their experiment the effects of word length and acoustic similarity on speech rate and serial recall performance were assessed in 4-, 7-, and 10-year-old children. The results of this experiment are shown in Fig. 2.3.

As can be seen in Fig. 2.3, children of different ages showed a word-length effect of equivalent size, and increases in recall with age were very well accounted for by increases in speech rate, as they had been in earlier studies (e.g. Hulme, Thomson, Muir, & Lawrence, 1984). In contrast to this, the absolute difference in recall between acoustically similar and dissimilar lists increased as children got older. This effect was also related to speech rate. Further analyses showed that the size of the difference in recall was correlated with speech rate, and this remained true even when the effects of age were partialled out. A second experiment, using a memory span procedure to avoid possible criticisms of range effects, confirmed this pattern of results in all important respects.

These results tell us a lot about the mechanisms underlying the acoustic similarity effect, and its development, and provide support for the importance of rehearsal as the basis of the effect. The relationship between speech rate and the size of the effect are particularly crucial in this respect and appear to tie the effect to the processes of rehearsal. This can be explained in the following way. Acoustically similar words will inevitably lead to the setting up of highly similar traces in the articulatory loop. It therefore follows that the traces of such sequences of items will be harder to discriminate one from another and, because the loop is subject to the loss of information due to decay over time, such loss of information will affect acoustically similar items more seriously than dissimilar ones.

A reasonable assumption is that errors are introduced at the point in time when items in the store are read and re-written into the store. Errors here are assumed to be based on guessing on the basis of partial information. As speech rate increases with increasing age, more items will be held on the loop, and inevitably more items will be read and re-written per unit of time. Because there are different error rates due to different levels of confusability, the absolute difference in recall between acoustically similar and dissimilar lists will increase.

This view of the acoustic similarity effect depending upon rehearsal is consistent with much other evidence that shows the effect is most pronounced in situations which provide most opportunities for rehearsal (Crowder, 1978); for example, Conrad (1967) showed that the size of the effect was decreased and eventually abolished if subjects were required to shadow irrelevant digits between presentation and recall. Similarly, Cowan, Cartwright, Winterowd, and Sherk (1987) set out to investigate the change in size of the acoustic similarity effect with age reported by Hulme (1984). They found, in a number of experiments, that adults, who recalled lists of spoken words following articulatory suppression, displayed patterns of recall similar to those of 5-year-old children. Furthermore, blocking rehearsal was more detrimental to the recall of dissimilar than similar lists. This, in a sense, is the converse of the developmental pattern, that as rehearsal speed increases, recall of dissimilar lists increases more than similar lists. Finally, in an unpublished study of our own with adult subjects, it was found that the introduction of an unfilled delay between presentation and recall (where rehearsal would be necessary to prevent forgetting) increased the size of the acoustic similarity effect. It did so in a particular way. Recall of dissimilar lists was unaffected by the delay, whereas recall of the similar lists was impaired. This, of course, is exactly what would be predicted by the view that the effect depends upon the misidentification of items during rehearsal.

This view might seem to conflict with evidence reviewed earlier showing that with articulatory suppression the acoustic similarity effect remains, albeit in an attenuated form. This, of course, is the pattern obtained by Cowan et al. (1987), and is perfectly consistent with the view advanced here. Provided that the materials are encoded into the loop, then, because acoustically similar lists comprise sequences of items that differ on few features, they will be recalled less well than dissimilar sequences where loss of distinctive features will be less crucial. In fact, the two-component view, which attributes the acoustic similarity effect to the passive input store, seems to have no explanation, without making further assumptions, as to why the size of the effect is attenuated by suppression.

The other issue is how the unattended speech effect is to be accounted for by a unitary view of the loop. In the unitary framework this effect can be explained by assuming that auditory speech input gains obligatory access to the loop (cf. explanations of the different effects of suppression depending on modality of input). The simultaneous input of items in the unattended speech experiments simply leads to problems of encoding the visually presented material onto the loop (the same argument has been advanced by Broadbent, 1984). This will also account for the interaction of this effect with articulatory suppression. With visual presentation the effect is abolished by suppression because this prevents encoding of items on to the loop (Salame & Baddeley, 1982). With auditory presentation, the effect survives the imposition of suppression (Hanley & C. Broadbent, 1987). This can be explained because the material gains obligatory access to the loop and the unattended speech causes interference with encoding.

In summary, it has been argued that a model of the articulatory loop as a unitary store may be more consistent with the available data from both developmental and adult studies, than the more complex two-component view advocated in Baddeley's (1986) latest refinement of the working memory model. The arguments here are admittedly a little complicated, but can perhaps be simplified to the following. In the Baddeley model there is a passive input store and this accounts for the acoustic similarity effect and the disruption caused in immediate memory experiments by hearing irrelevant speech. The information in this passive store can be refreshed by a process of rehearsal and it is this process that brings about the system's sensitivity to the effects of word length.

In contrast, we have argued that there is just one store to hold information in an articulatory code. The effects of word length and acoustic similarity place limits on this store in different ways. Long words are rehearsed more slowly and so fewer can be rehearsed within the decay time of the store (so we are in agreement with Baddeley's explanation of this effect). Acoustically similar and dissimilar items are rehearsed just as quickly as each other, but the similar items are more likely to be confused because they differ by fewer articulatory features. Because acoustically similar items have similar articulatory traces, any loss of information due to decay affects them more adversely than acoustically dissimilar items. It is proposed that this loss of discriminability results in errors occurring during the rehearsal process (and also during retrieval at recall). It is proposed that these errors arise from guessing based on the partial cues that are available concerning an item.

We will argue later in the book that this unitary view is also better able to cope with some of the results of our studies of the articulatory loop in people with severe learning difficulties.

THE CENTRAL EXECUTIVE AND THE STORAGE OF NON-PHONOLOGICAL INFORMATION

The central executive in the Baddeley and Hitch model is considered to function as a control system. It is a limited capacity, attentional system, responsible for co-ordinating the input and output of information to and from the subsidiary slave systems, and for selecting and operating control processes and strategies. It is, therefore, both a very complex and inherently slightly vague construct, one which Baddeley (1983) himself has said "could, not unfairly, be described as the area of residual ignorance".

One aspect of the central executive which seems problematic to us is that, at times, it is assigned a storage as well as a control function. However, the parameters governing its storage abilities are left completely unspecified. For these reasons we should prefer to see the central executive confined to an attentional and controlling function.

One example of storage, that is sometimes attributed to the central executive, is the residual component of recall left when subjects are performing articulatory suppression. As described earlier, suppression dramatically impairs serial recall performance, but it far from abolishes it. Typically, memory span is reduced from 7–8 items to about 3–4 items under suppression. This residual span is clearly not dependent upon speech coding, because it is insensitive to the effects of word length and acoustic similarity, Thus, within the Baddeley and Hitch working memory model it has been attributed to the operation of the central executive.

There is, to our minds, a more natural locus for such storage of information in a non-phonological form; an obvious hypothesis is that it depends upon activation of information in long-term, or secondary, memory. The idea of long-term storage contributing to immediate serial recall performance is not mentioned in the working memory model. However, there is a diverse body of work which provides support for the importance of such a contribution.

Support for this view comes from studies of the effects of word frequency on short-term memory performance. Watkins (1977) found that span was higher if high-frequency words made up the first part of a list rather than low-frequency words; showing that recall of items early in a list reflects the operation of a mechanism sensitive to word frequency. He argued that this effect depended upon rehearsal of the early items in the list, high-frequency words being more easily transferred into long-term memory. However, it may be that Watkins' results could be explained in terms of the operation of the articulatory loop. Wright (1979) showed that high-frequency words were articulated more rapidly than low-frequency words. He went on to argue that the advantage of lists containing high-frequency words in early positions could be due to the maintenance and retrieval of early items from the articulatory loop. Gregg, Freedman, and Smith (1989), however, showed that although suppression removes some of the effects of word frequency on memory span (those that are due to the articulatory loop and articulation rate), even with suppression memory span is greater for lists of high- than low-frequency words. Such effects evidently reflect the operation of a memory store that is sensitive to the effects of word frequency, as long-term memory is known to be.

Another sort of evidence comes from an old experiment by Hebb (1961). He showed that with repetition of supra-span lists, immediate serial recall improved over trials, implying that the creation of long-term memory representations of the word sequences had occurred. A natural implication of this is that, normally, recall of lists at or near span may be partially dependent on such long-term memory representations.

One other thread of evidence that is consistent with this argument comes from neuropsychology (for a review of such evidence see Baddeley, 1986). Some patients with short-term memory impairments fail to show evidence of word-length or phonological similarity effects, indicating the abolition of phonological coding (this perhaps is analogous to the state of affairs in normal subjects who are required to suppress articulation). Saffran and Marin (1975) proposed long-term memory as the basis for this residual capacity, as their short-term memory patient's performance resembled delayed rather than immediate recall. Their patient showed a primacy but no recency effect and his repetition was sensitive to familiarity and meaningfulness of the words used.

Finally, in some recent experiments Hulme et al., (1991) set out to test the importance of a long-term memory contribution to memory span. In the first experiment, non-words were used because they lack a long-term memory representation. Memory span was lower for non-words than for words, and in both cases a linear function related recall to speech rate for items of differing spoken durations. The function for non-words had an equivalent slope (interpreted as reflecting a contribution from the articulatory loop) but a lower intercept (interpreted as reflecting a contribution from long-term memory). The second experiment compared memory span for Italian and English words. Span was lower for Italian than English words, due to a depression in the intercept of the recall speech-rate function, but learning the English translations of these words increased subjects' memory span for them. These results therefore provide some direct support for the idea that memory span depends to quite a substantial degree upon information in long-term memory. Hulme et al. argued that it was long-term memory for the phonological form of words that was particularly crucial in this respect.

In summary, a common theme in these different lines of evidence is that once the markers for speech coding in the articulatory loop have been removed, there remains a residual contribution to memory span. This contribution, we have argued, is much more parsimoniously attributed to the operation of long-term memory than to the central executive of the working memory model.

SUMMARY: THE STRUCTURE OF WORKING MEMORY

We began with a very general definition of working memory as the system (or systems) responsible for the temporary storage of information during more complex cognitive tasks. We moved on from this to consider the most detailed attempt to give a structural model of the working memory system: The work of Baddeley and Hitch. As will be evident from this presentation there may be a number of specific issues that are the subject of some controversy. It is worth emphasizing, however, that the success of the model is not in any way crucial to the acceptance of the importance of the concept of working memory. Such a concept seems central to much work in cognitive psychology at present. The Baddeley and Hitch model is important as an attempt to give a detailed specification of the operation of working memory. Specific details of the model might, however, be rejected without questioning the need for such a concept. The work described here has been concerned with the structural properties of working memory, not with assessing the importance of working memory as a functional concept.

In our presentation of this model we have focused on certain aspects of it which seem questionable to us. These criticisms, clearly, are matters of detail that we hope will contribute to a refinement of this general approach. One point which emerges with great clarity from all of this work is the importance of some form of articulatory coding in the performance of traditional short-term memory tasks. This has been explained in terms of the articulatory loop. One point of debate here is whether it is necessary to divide the loop into two separate components. It has been argued that a more parsimonious unitary model of the loop accommodates current findings most adequately. In Chapter 5, we will present an examination of the effects of word length and acoustic similarity on short-term memory in children with severe learning difficulties. In discussing those studies we will again argue in favour of a unitary model of the articulatory loop.

A second point of controversy has concerned the role of the central executive. The main role of the central executive is as an attentional control system responsible for managing the operation of the memory system. Whether such a system should also be attributed a storage function seems debatable. Baddeley himself has recently expressed reservations about this idea (personal communication). We have argued that, in fact, effects that have sometimes been attributed to the storage capacity of the central executive are better seen as signs of the role of long-term memory processes.

Finally, it may be appropriate to emphasize the continuity between the working memory approach and earlier work. In many ways the working memory model of Baddeley and Hitch can be seen as a development of the modal model. It is not so much that the concept of a short-term store, as embodied in the modal model, was wrong; just that it was incomplete in important respects. The working memory model can be seen as an attempt to develop earlier models of short-term memory to account for a greater variety of findings. The model has certainly been outstandingly successful as framework for recent studies of short-term memory phenomena. Indeed, a cynic might argue that even in research conducted within this framework, the role of working memory as a determinant of performance on other more complex tasks has again slipped into the background. With few exceptions (such as Hitch's work on mental arithmetic) experiments within this tradition have concentrated on more and more fine-grained analyses of short-term memory phenomena and have paid little attention to the possible roles of this system in more complex tasks. We will return to this issue (a criticism to which the present work is far from immune) in the final chapter.

CHAPTER 3

Working Memory Development, Cognitive Development, and Learning Difficulties

In the previous chapter we considered the concept of working memory, and focused particularly on the Baddeley and Hitch working memory model. This model provides a framework for some of the experiments presented later, dealing with explanations of the memory deficits found in children with learning difficulties. In the present chapter we consider previous work concerned with the development of short-term memory skills in children and the impairments of these processes found in severe learning difficulties.

WHY DOES MEMORY SPAN INCREASE WITH AGE?

The growth of memory span with age is often taken as evidence of a general increase in the ability to take in, hold, and handle information. Thus, when asking why memory span increases, we are also asking why or how does information processing capacity in short-term memory increase. To talk of capacity increasing suggests an increase in storage space in short-term memory, but the evidence we will review here suggests that storage capacity does not change, but rather it is processing efficiency that improves with age. Research described in

Chapter 2 showed that short-term memory limitations in adults are related to articulation rate, which provides an index of how fast words can be rehearsed in the articulatory loop. One important question, therefore, is whether this can be applied to the dramatic increases in memory span seen in normal development. Before considering this question we will consider some of the other major attempts to explain why memory span increases with age.

Strategy Production Deficiencies

One explanation which has been applied widely in studies of memory development is the increased use of strategies with age (Flavell, 1970, 1977). Strategies are intentional, goal-directed, procedures; memory strategies are things we choose to do to help us remember. In this view, increases in memory performance with age, are due to children using memory strategies more efficiently as they get older. The two most studied strategies are rehearsal and organization. We shall consider each in turn.

Rehearsal

A classic study used to support the importance of rehearsal is that of Flavell, Beach, and Chinsky (1966). They looked at the performance of 5-, 7-, and 10-year-olds in a visual memory task and were particularly concerned with whether these children were naming pictures as an aid to recalling them. Older children did show more sign of lip movements (taken as evidence of verbal rehearsal) than the younger children. In a further experiment (Keeney, Cannizzo, & Flavell, 1967), using the same task, recall was found to be better in 6- and 7-year-old children showing signs of rehearsal than in "non-rehearsers". Keeney et al. also found that training non-rehearsers to name and rehearse the names of the pictures improved their performance to the level of those already using rehearsal. They argued from this that young children are not unable to name pictures or use verbal rehearsal, but that they may be reluctant to use these strategies; this is what is meant by a "production deficiency".

If the use of rehearsal is the reason for improvements in memory performance with age, training to rehearse should improve recall in younger children, but not older children or adults who are already using rehearsal. Indeed, if we were to take a strong line on the importance of rehearsal or other strategies as determinants of developmental improvements on short-term memory tasks, then training such strategies should eliminate age differences on these tasks. Keeney et al. (1967) found that training the non-rehearsers improved their recall to the same level as the rehearsers. However, this was not a developmental study, so it was not possible to show differential effects of rehearsal training in different age groups.

There are further complications in trying to use these studies to furnish an explanation for developmental increases in short-term memory skills. These studies used visual memory tasks, where the child has the extra demand of re-coding the pictures into verbal form in order to rehearse their names. There was also a delay between presentation of the pictures and the child being allowed to recall their names. More typical measures of short-term memory, such as the digit-span tests used in IQ batteries, use auditory presentation and immediate verbal recall. There is no re-coding necessary and recall is not delayed. Nevertheless, such tasks show dramatic developmental improvements.

If we consider these task differences between the typical memory span task, digit span, and the Flavell picture-recall task they cast doubt on the usefulness of rehearsal as an explanation for developmental improvements in short-term memory skills. Hitch and Halliday (1983) and Hulme et al. (1984) have found word-length effects in verbal serial recall, which suggests verbal rehearsal, in children as young as 4 and 5 years (these experiments are discussed later in this chapter). There is evidence that the use of rehearsal for visual memory tasks develops later than the use of rehearsal in auditory memory tasks (Hitch & Halliday, 1983). As digit span is an auditory memory task our understanding of increases in memory span with age needs to be based on studies of auditory memory.

A further point is that rehearsal differences do not seem capable of explaining the differences in short-term memory performance that exist between adults. Lyon (1977), using auditory presentation, found that prevention of rehearsal (by presenting items very fast) had a similar effect on the recall of adults with good memory spans and adults with poor memory spans. When both groups could not rehearse, the group with good memory spans were still performing better than the group with poor memory spans. These results do not show rehearsal to be unimportant developmentally. It would, however, be preferable if the explanation for developmental differences in memory span made contact with explanations for individual differences in span that exist amongst adults. The explanation put forward later, in terms of articulation speed, succeeds in this respect.

There are many other studies of rehearsal and the development of this strategy in young children (for a review see Kail, 1984). It is not appropriate to consider these studies in detail here. It should be stressed, however, that rehearsal training has not been shown to be capable of reducing or eliminating age differences on traditional short-term memory tasks such as digit span. This is not to say that changes in rehearsal have no part to play in explaining age differences in short-term memory performance. The inefficient use of rehearsal by young children may well contribute to poor performance on some memory tasks; possibly particularly on visually presented tasks where there is a significant delay between presentation and recall (see for example, Hulme, Silvester, Smith, & Muir, 1986, for further discussion of this issue). Changes in rehearsal cannot, however, take us far in explaining the dramatic improvements with age seen on immediate serial recall tasks, such as digit span.

Organization

An alternative explanation for increasing span is that the child is increasingly able to organize input into "chunks" (Simon, 1974). It was suggested (Miller, 1956) that short-term memory capacity was related to the number of "chunks" that could be held in short-term memory at any one time. Simon's hypothesis was that children do not organize or group material and, therefore, do not put as much information into a "chunk", as adults do. It was noted above that this conception of short-term memory does not fit recent evidence, in particular the word-length effect.

However, it is known that material that is organized (either externally or internally) is recalled better than unorganized material (Tulving & Donaldson, 1972). If one takes the extreme view, that an increase in organizational ability is responsible for performance differences with age, then imposed organization should eliminate differences in performance. A less extreme view, that organization contributes to improvements in memory performance with age, would still require training studies showing that grouping produced larger improvements in younger than older children in order to support it.

Huttenlocher and Burke (1976) looked at recall of digits which were grouped or ungrouped, in four age groups (4, 7, 9, and 11 years old). Their results showed that grouping had an equivalent, and beneficial, effect on recall in all age groups. This casts strong doubt on the relevance of grouping to any explanation of developmental differences in memory span performance. Similarly, grouping does not provide an explanation for individual differences in memory span found amongst adults. Lyon (1977), comparing adults with high and low memory spans, found that grouping material had the same beneficial effect on recall in both groups.

Engle and Marshall (1983) looked at memory span for grouped and ungrouped digits in 6-year-olds, 12-year-olds, and adults. They found that grouping improved performance in all groups when presentation was slow (1 digit per second), but only in the two older groups when presentation was fast (2.5 digits per second). Engle and Marshall felt that although rehearsal was possible at the slow presentation rate, it was difficult when digits were presented fast. With slow presentation there was some evidence of a differential effect of grouping: Reducing (but not eliminating) the difference in memory span between the adults and 12-year-olds, but increasing the difference between the 6- and 12-year-olds. This pattern was not found when fast presentation was used; the memory span of adults improved even more than that of 12-year-olds and the performance of 6-year-olds appeared not to be improved by grouping. In this instance, grouping increased differences in levels of memory span performance, rather than reducing them. The finding that different presentation rates had different effects, was attributed to different rehearsal abilities and possibilities. Thus, Engle and Marshall (1983) did find a differential effect of experimenter- imposed grouping, but only with slow presentation and between 12-year-olds and adults. They conclude that memory span differences cannot be explained by a single factor, such as the use of a strategy like grouping.

The evidence on organization and rehearsal suggests that although both improve performance on short-term memory tests, they have similar effects on subjects of different ages and abilities. It seems unlikely that a production deficiency, or a decision not to use a specific strategy, can account either for differences in memory span found amongst adults or for the gradual increase in memory span from childhood to adulthood.

Efficiency of Basic Processes

We have considered explanations of short-term memory development in terms of strategy changes and found them lacking. What then are the alternatives? The most prominent class of alternative explanations considers that instead of differences arising from changes in strategies, they arise from differences in the efficiency with which certain basic memory processes can be carried out. The most studied measures of the efficiency of basic processes have focused on measuring simple, some might say trivial, responses with an emphasis on how quickly the subject can perform the task. Performance on these speeded tasks is then related to variations in performance on memory tasks.

Rate of Trace Decay

In tests of short-term retention it has generally been agreed that memory traces are labile and rapidly fade if not refreshed or re-activated by an active strategy such as rehearsal. Perhaps the first example of an explanation of short-term memory development, in terms of changes in basic processes, proposed that in younger children, the rate of trace decay may be faster. Belmont (1972) showed that this is not the case. He found that immediate recall in young children was worse than in older subjects; even at zero delay (immediate recall) children recall less than adults. However, after controlling for the level of initial recall, he found that children's rate of forgetting (as shown by the fall in recall over increasing intervals) was similar to that of adults. It appears that the rate of trace decay is the same in children and adults, but as the level of performance at zero delay is poorer in children than in adults, some other factor must be limiting performance in children.

Item Identification
One of the first demonstrations of the usefulness of looking at changes in basic processes to explain developmental improvements in short-term memory was the work of Case, Kurland, and Goldberg (1982). They argued that improvements in memory span with age were attributable to increasing "operational efficiency". The particular process, or operation, studied by Case et al. was the speed of item identification. They measured the time between the presentation of a word and the start of the subject's verbal reproduction of it. The time taken to begin to say the single syllable words used in the experiment decreased between the ages of 3 to 6 years. There was, in fact, a linear relationship between memory span and response time, such that as response time decreased with age, memory span increased. Case et al. considered that the voice onset time measure they used was essentially a measure of item identification time. They interpreted their results in terms of a trade-off between the attentional capacity required for item identification and item storage. As the operational efficiency of item identification increases, more attentional capacity is available for the storage of items.

Articulation Speed
An alternative approach to explaining developmental changes in short-term memory arose from the working memory model. According to this approach the use of the articulatory loop in serial recall suggests two factors which could relate to improved memory span with age. These two factors are the length of the articulatory loop and the speed at which information is re-cycled or rehearsed. Either, or both, of these might change in the course of normal development, and a change of either type would be expected to lead to changes in short-term memory performance.

There are now a number of developmental studies that have investigated these possibilities by relating recall to articulation speed for words of different spoken lengths in children of different ages (Hitch

& Halliday, 1983; Hulme & Muir, 1985; Hulme & Tordoff, 1989; Hulme et al., 1984; Nicolson, 1981).

Nicolson (1981), using visual presentation, looked at the effect of word length on serial recall in groups of children aged 8, 10, and 12 years. Young children could not be included in this study because of the need for all children to be able to read the words used in the experiment. All groups showed the same word-length effect, serial recall of short words (with fast articulation time) was better than that of long words (slow articulation time). There was an increase in both articulation rate and serial recall with increasing age. Nicolson found that 8- to 12-year-olds showed the same linear relationship between articulation rate and memory span as found by Baddeley et al. (1975) for adults.

Hitch and Halliday (1983) looked at the word-length effect in groups of children aged 6, 8, and 10 years using both pictures and spoken words (visual and auditory presentation). All ages showed an effect on recall of word length with auditory presentation. As in Nicholson's study there was an increase in speech rate with age and this closely paralleled the increase in recall scores.

Finally, Hulme et al., (1984) related recall to speech rate for words of different lengths over a very wide age range: In 4-, 7-, and 11-year-olds and adults. Words of one, two, and three syllables were chosen from pre-reading books, so as to be familiar to even the youngest children, and speech rate was assessed by repetition of word pairs, from each of the word pools used in the experiment. The results of this study are shown in Fig. 3.1, where recall is plotted against speech rate for all age groups.

These results are striking in that the same linear function relating recall to speech rate fits the results for all age groups. Subjects of different ages in this study all recalled, on average, as much as they could say in roughly 1.5 seconds. Increases in memory span with age are seen to be very closely related to changes in speech rate with age.

Thus the results of these different studies are remarkably clear and consistent. The dramatic improvements in serial recall performance with increasing age are closely and quantitatively related to changes in speech rate. In terms of the articulatory loop theory, which gave impetus to these studies, the length of the loop appears to remain constant across different ages; more material is stored in this system because it can be spoken and so rehearsed more rapidly.

These results, relating developmental increases in speech rate to increases in short-term memory efficiency, lead quite directly to a simple causal theory: That increases in memory span with age depend upon increases in speech rate. Needless to say, however, such a theory is not necessitated by the findings. The findings are essentially correlational;

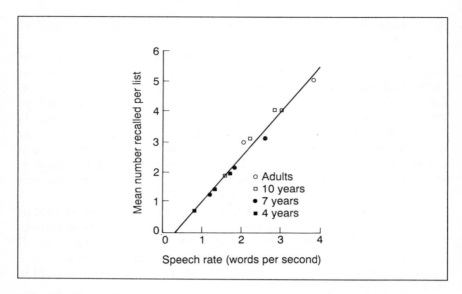

FIG. 3.1. Mean number of words recalled per list versus speech rates for adults, 10-, 7-, and 4-year-old children. (From Hulme et al., 1984.)

as children get older their speech rate increases and in line with this so does their memory performance. It could be that both these changes depend upon some other factor. The obvious way to test this causal theory is to conduct a training study. If short-term memory depends upon speech rate, if we can successfully train children to speak faster, then this should, according to the theory, lead to a corresponding increase in short-term memory.

Hulme and Muir (1985) set out to test this hypothesis. Two experiments were conducted with 7-year-old children, in which it was attempted to train them to say the words used in the memory task more quickly. In this study, only tiny changes in speech rate were observed in the children who were trained to speak faster and, unfortunately, these increases were not reliably larger than in control children, who had equivalent exposure to the words, without any emphasis on saying them quickly. This negative result is ambiguous. If speech rate had increased substantially, without affecting recall, this would have effectively disproved the theory. The failure to improve either speech rate or recall, however, gets us no further forward. It could be that with more extensive training, speech rate would have increased. The impression gained during this study, however, was that speech rate would not be easy to increase by training. Perhaps this should not surprise us; we get massive practice in this skill and it shows gradual improvement over a very long period of development. Brief, intensive training, is probably not going to effect any changes in the skill that we are interested in. If this is true, the causal theory becomes very difficult to test.

Most recently, Raine, Hulme, Chadderton, and Bailey (1991) have tried to explore this causal theory about the relationship between articulation rate and memory span in children with speech disorders. The theory predicts that children with pathologically slow speech will show reduced short-term memory capacity. Raine et al. set out to test this, by selecting children undergoing speech therapy who were considered to show marked impairments in their rate of speech in the absence of any significant receptive language difficulties. The speech disordered group had a variety of diagnosed difficulties. The purest, and theoretically most interesting group, were 12 children suffering from dysarthria (slow speech due to neurological damage to the speech musculature). Another small group had developmental verbal dyspraxia, a condition involving the retarded development of the processes necessary for the selection, programming, and execution of articulatory gestures in the absence of any peripheral impairments. The final group of children had a variety of less clear-cut difficulties including immature language and phonological disorder. These children's short-term memory performance was compared with that of a group of normal control children, individually matched for age and sex. Receptive language skills for all children were assessed with the English Picture Vocabulary Test, a test of naming ability that correlates highly with verbal IQ. Spatial skills were assessed with the picture completion test from the WISC, a measure of visuo-perceptual ability.

One obvious problem in assessing verbal memory performance in such a group of children with speech difficulties, is that their slow speech may hinder their performance in a task involving a verbal response. In order to overcome this problem, the children's short-term memory skills were tested using a variation on a memory task involving sequences of nameable pictures, and requiring a non-verbal response (Hulme et al. 1986). Hulme et al. found that memory for short-named pictures was greater than for long-named pictures, reflecting the use of the articulatory loop, by normal children, in this task.

The results of this experiment were straightforward, and provided good support for the theory linking developments in short-term memory capacity to improvements in articulatory speed with age. The speech disordered children had lower short-term memory spans, and showed smaller word-length effects, and less evidence of speech motor activity during rehearsal periods, than the normal children. Covariance analyses showed that these differences were not a function of differences in intelligence or motor speed between the groups. Furthermore, using speech rate as a covariate actually abolished the group difference in short-term memory span between the groups. In other words, statistically eliminating differences in speech rate between the groups, eliminated the differences in memory span. Finally, a separate analysis of the children with dysarthria (a relatively pure group, with peripheral problems in the control of the speech musculature) showed exactly the same pattern. The overall pattern of results here is, therefore, consistent with the idea that speech rate is a causal determinant of verbal memory span. It is still possible that these results reflect some other difference between the speech disordered and normal children apart from speech rate. If such a factor exists, it would seem in any case to be closely related to speech rate. Further studies which follow children with speech disorders undergoing speech therapy might help to clarify the picture. If it could be shown that increases in articulation speed in these children, following speech therapy, are paralleled by equivalent improvements in short-term memory, this would provide even stronger support for the theory.

Articulation Speed versus Item Identification Speed

There is a great deal of evidence linking changes in short-term memory to changes in speech rate with age. We must consider, in a little more detail, the interpretation of these effects. One obvious question is the relationship between articulation rate and the item identification speed measure used by Case et al. (1982).

It has been argued before that the repetition of single words, or small groups of words, as measured in our own experiments, provides a measure of articulation rate that is independent of the time taken for item recognition (Hulme et al. 1984). In contrast, the measure used by Case et al. (1982) could be viewed as a composite of item-recognition and speech-onset time. The fact that there is such a substantial relationship between memory span and articulation speed would seem to show that the item identification measure used by Case et al. is not the relevant determinant of increases in span with age. Instead, rate of articulation, would seem to provide a better explanation for increases in span with age. In this view, the success of the measure used by Case et al. depends on it providing a rough measure of articulation speed, as well as item identification speed.

The most direct test of these alternatives was provided by Hitch, Halliday, and Littler (1989). They measured memory span for one, two, and three syllable words in 8- and 11-year-old children. They also obtained measures of articulation rate and word identification time for the words used in the experiment. Their results showed that articulation rate was an excellent predictor of memory span for the different materials, as it was in the earlier studies just described. Item identification time proved to be a much poorer predictor of memory span. Hitch et al. also showed that articulatory suppression, which is known to block rehearsal in the articulatory loop, abolished the effects of word length on memory span. We have also obtained such a result with presentation of pictures to children between the ages of 4 and 10 (Hulme et al., 1986). These results fit well with the idea of an articulatory rehearsal process underlying the effects of word length but would be difficult to reconcile with the idea that word-length effects are mediated by differences in the speed of item identification.

SUMMARY: WHY MEMORY SPAN INCREASES WITH AGE

We have considered possible explanations for the dramatic improvements in short-term memory span that occur during development. The most successful explanation to date draws on the idea of an articulatory loop, as embodied in the working memory model. It would seem that there is no increase in the capacity of this system with age, but that there are large increases in articulation speed. These increases in articulation speed enable more information to be rehearsed within the decay time of the loop, so increasing the amount that can be stored. There is a close, quantitative relationship between the changes in articulation rate that occur with increasing age and the increases in memory span that are observed. The relationship between articulation rate and memory span provides an explanation for variations in span across individuals both within and across age groups, and across different types of materials (words of different lengths). There is no doubt that an explanation of short-term memory improvements in terms of increases in articulation rate with age is by far the most successful explanation to date. It should be stressed, however, that this causal theory is so far based on purely correlational evidence. We cannot say that the proposed causal link between improvements in articulatory skills with age, and changes in short-term memory, has yet been demonstrated conclusively. Nevertheless, this theory provides the first explanation, in quantitative terms, for the growth of short-term memory span with age and it also provides an explanation for the individual differences in span that exist within all age groups, including adults. It is now time to consider possible explanations of the short-term memory impairments found in people with severe learning difficulties, in the light of these ideas about the normal development of short-term memory.

WORKING MEMORY AND LEARNING DIFFICULTIES

There is a great deal of evidence that people with severe learning difficulties show considerable impairments of short-term memory. We will consider some of this evidence here. In the light of the ideas about working memory we discussed in Chapter 2, these problems of short-term memory may assume a new importance. If the short-term retention of verbal information is important in a range of educationally important skills, such comprehending and producing language, reading, arithmetic, and reasoning, problems of short-term memory may contribute significantly to the pervasive cognitive deficits shown in those with severe learning difficulties.

SHORT-TERM MEMORY DEFICITS AND SEVERE LEARNING DIFFICULTIES

We shall begin by considering studies of memory span in relation to other mental abilities in Down's syndrome people and others with severe learning difficulties.

The Illinois Test of Psycholinguistic Abilities (ITPA) has 12 sub-tests for different abilities related to language, including a digit span test. Marinosson (1974) compared normal children's performance on the ITPA with that of people with mild and severe learning difficulties, all matched for mental age (MA = 5 years). The two short-term memory tests (auditory and visual serial recall) stood out as the tests where performance decreased significantly with lower levels of intelligence. On the auditory sequential memory test (digit span), normal children performed significantly better than both groups with learning difficulties, as they also did on the visual sequential memory test (which requires short-term retention of meaningless symbols).

There are similar studies of ITPA profiles for Down's syndrome groups. Bilovsky and Share (1965) found that digit span performance is poor compared to the level of performance on the other sub-tests and measured against the normal profile of test performance. This study did not include a control group of other people with learning difficulties. Rempel (1974) compared matched groups of Down's syndrome people and others with learning difficulties, and found that the digit span of the Down's syndrome group was poor in relation to that of the non-Down's subjects with learning difficulties.

It has been suggested that short-term memory problems, in Down's syndrome in particular, relate to retrieval rather than storage problems (Dodd, 1975; McDade & Adler, 1980). Dodd (1975) compared recognition memory and reproduction of words in Down's syndrome children and others with severe learning difficulties of the same mental age. She found that recognition memory was similar in the two groups, but that the Down's group were poorer than her other subjects on the reproduction of words. McDade and Adler (1980) compared Down's syndrome and mental age matched normal children on tests of visual and auditory sequential memory. They tested auditory serial memory under two main conditions, recall and recognition. In the recall condition subjects had to reproduce the sequence verbally, but in the recognition test an array of pictures were shown and the subject pointed to the pictures of the items spoken in the test sequence. McDade and Adler found no difference in the recognition memory of the Down's syndrome and mental age (MA) matched normal children. However, there was a difference in serial recall performance, when subjects were asked to reproduce the sequence (as in a digit span test), with the performance of the Down's syndrome group being below that of the MA matched normal group. Both Dodd (1975) and McDade and Adler (1980) interpret their findings as evidence of a retrieval deficit in short-term auditory memory in Down's syndrome, because recognition was similar to matched groups but reproduction was not.

To summarize, there is evidence of poor auditory serial recall in people with learning difficulties (Marinosson, 1974) and Down's syndrome (Dodd, 1975; McDade & Adler, 1980). These studies of memory span in Down's syndrome people and others with learning difficulties have always compared groups at one level of mental development. Memory span is known to increase with age in normal development, and this has been the focus of much of the research that was discussed earlier. However, nothing is known about memory span at different stages of development in Down's syndrome people or others with severe learning difficulties. This indicates a need for developmental studies of memory span performance in Down's syndrome people and others with severe learning difficulties. We will present the first study of this type in Chapter 4.

EXPLANATIONS OF SHORT-TERM MEMORY DEFICITS ASSOCIATED WITH LEARNING DIFFICULTIES

Explanations of short-term memory deficits associated with learning difficulties have been closely related to explanations of normal memory development. Research has largely been dominated by work on strategies such as rehearsal and organization. Alternative explanations of memory span development, such as that based on articulation rate and the concept of the articulatory loop, have not been applied to those with learning difficulties. Most of the research concerned with short-term memory deficits has been conducted with subjects with moderate learning difficulties; there is a widespread, if implicit, assumption that explanations will generalize to those with severe learning difficulties. This is perhaps a reasonable assumption, but one that has yet to be properly tested.

Stimulus Trace

The earliest explanation of short-term memory deficits in those with learning difficulties was that the "traces" of sensory stimuli were less strong and faded more quickly than they did in normal subjects (N. R. Ellis, 1963). Ellis needed to show that recall performance of those with learning difficulties was particularly bad in delayed response tasks, as compared to immediate recall. However, the evidence from Belmont (1972) shows that their recall was below that of normal groups at zero delay (immediate recall) and that the fall in recall as delay increases (the rate of forgetting) is the same as that of normal subjects matched for mental age. No neurological evidence has been found to support the idea of poor stimulus traces in those with learning difficulties, and N. R. Ellis (1978) has himself revised his opinion on their short-term memory problems.

Strategies and Control Processes

N. R. Ellis (1978) argued that the short-term memory deficits of those with learning difficulties are best described in terms of their use of control processes, rather than any differences in storage space or capacity in the memory system. This view was based largely on the highly influential work of Belmont and Butterfield (1969, 1971) which in turn drew on earlier work on strategies as an explanation of normal short-term memory development.

Belmont and Butterfield (1969) investigated the use of strategies, in groups of normal people and those with moderate learning difficulties, matched for mental age, in a visual memory experiment where subjects were able to set the pace of item presentation. Subjects in the normal group left gaps between items, with particularly long gaps after three items. Belmont and Butterfield interpreted this as evidence of the use of rehearsal between items, and the grouping of items into rehearsal sets of three. Those with moderate learning difficulties did not show this pattern, preferring fast presentation (short gaps) throughout the sequence. Belmont and Butterfield concluded that these subjects failed to use either rehearsal or organization.

In subsequent experiments, Belmont and Butterfield (1971) showed that after training in the use of these active strategies the performance of those with learning difficulties increased to match that of the mental age matched normal subjects. Unfortunately, however, they did not give equivalent training to the normal children who allegedly were already using organization and rehearsal to facilitate their memory performance. It would have been much more convincing if it could have been shown that such training had no (or at least less) effect in the normal children. Nevertheless, it would seem that one source of the deficit of those with learning difficulties on this visual memory task is a failure to use appropriate strategies. This view of short-term memory deficits as failure to spontaneously use strategies has been widely accepted and has generated much research on strategy training programmes in those with moderate learning difficulties (for example, Brown, Campione, & Murphy, 1974). This view of memory deficits, based on studies of visual memory in moderate learning difficulties, has been generalized to those with severe learning difficulties and applied to their education (Rectory Paddock School, 1981).

There are, however, problems in accepting this evidence for deficient strategy use in those with moderate learning difficulties as a sufficient explanation for their wide ranging short-term memory problems. These problems largely parallel the problems of interpretation surrounding the studies of strategy differences in children of different ages discussed earlier.

The first point is that these tasks involve visual presentation, which may involve at least partially different processes to auditory tasks such as digit span. There is evidence that people with learning difficulties are not as ready as normal children to recode visual information into a temporal, or verbal code (O'Connor & Hermelin, 1973). O'Connor and Hermelin presented three digits (visually) in such a way that they varied in their spatial order (left to right) and also their temporal order (first to last). They found that many of those with severe learning difficulties recognized the digits in their spatial order (as did deaf children) rather than in their temporal order. Normal children of the same mental age consistently recognized the digits in their temporal order. O'Connor and Hermelin consider that the re-coding of visual information into a temporal, successive order, is an important aspect of normal short-term memory. The failure of those with severe learning difficulties in this experiment to use a temporal code may be evidence of a failure to derive or evoke a verbal representation of visual material (O'Connor & Hermelin, 1978). Clearly, if information is not recoded in verbal form it is not possible for the subject to use verbal rehearsal.

One final point concerning the role of rehearsal in explaining the short-term memory problems of those with severe learning difficulties concerns the extent to which rehearsal training produces memory improvements. In many studies rehearsal training produces improvements in short-term memory but there are almost always residual impairments, even in comparison to younger normal children of the same mental age. So, rehearsal training does not even bring the short-term memory skills of those with learning difficulties up to the low level expected on the basis of their other cognitive abilities. The conclusion that seems justifiable closely parallels the one we reached when considering the role of rehearsal as an explanation for memory improvements in normal development: Rehearsal may play a role in explaining the memory deficits but it seems far from a complete and satisfactory explanation in itself. It would certainly seem worthwhile looking at basic processes in the hope that a more adequate explanation of the memory deficits in severe learning difficulties can be found. It is always possible that deficiencies in basic processes (such as difficulties in naming visual stimuli or poor articulation skills) could in turn produce failures to use rehearsal.

SUMMARY AND CONCLUSIONS: WORKING MEMORY PROCESSES AND LEARNING DIFFICULTIES

From this brief and selective review of short-term memory in people with learning difficulties a number of important questions emerge. The first issues are descriptive. We know that learning difficulties are associated with short-term memory problems. In fact, the deficit on short-term memory tasks is more severe than on some other tasks because the deficit is present when comparing people with severe learning difficulties with younger normal children of the same mental age (MA). We know almost nothing about the developmental pattern of short-term memory in severe learning difficulties, however. In normal children memory span develops with chronological age and by definition this development occurs alongside increases in MA. In severe learning difficulties, however, mental age lags behind chronological age. One question, therefore, is whether or not short-term memory development keeps pace even with the slower pace of development in MA shown in people with learning difficulties. Another descriptive issue is whether all those with severe learning difficulties show equivalent short-term memory deficits. In particular, we wish to know whether those with Down's syndrome differ from other people with severe learning difficulties in the extent of their short-term memory problems or the changes in short-term memory shown with increasing chronological and mental age. These are the issues we shall address in Chapter 4.

The other issues are more theoretical. It is clear that we lack a convincing account of the deficits shown by those with severe learning difficulties on auditory short-term memory tasks such as digit span. Explanations to date have stressed the role of strategy differences. There are difficulties with this sort of explanation when applied either to normal short-term memory development or to the deficits shown in severe learning difficulties. There is a clear gulf between our current understanding of short-term memory deficits in severe learning difficulties and recent studies of the processes responsible for the development of short-term memory in normal children. In particular, the most successful theory in accounting for improvements in short-term memory has drawn on the concept of the articulatory loop, and the role of increases in the rate of articulation, as an explanation for improvements in short-term memory with age. It is well recognized that articulation skills are poor in those with severe learning difficulties, particularly in Down's syndrome (Benda, 1969). It would seem natural, therefore, to explore the relationship between articulation rate and short-term memory in severe learning difficulties. We present the first studies of this sort in Chapter 5.

The final set of issues that follow on from these descriptive and theoretical questions are of more applied interest. In view of the possible role of short-term memory as a working memory system, it seems possible that an understanding of the deficits on short-term memory tasks shown by those with severe learning difficulties will help us to explain their difficulties in mastering some other cognitive skills. These people have demonstrable impairments in language skills and in learning a range of educationally important skills, such as reading and arithmetic. A better understanding of the short-term memory problems in severe learning difficulties might, it is hoped, shed light on these more general educational difficulties.

CHAPTER 4

Memory Span Development in Severe Learning Difficulties

The research reviewed in the previous chapter was concerned with the characteristics of short-term memory performance in children with Down's syndrome and other groups of children with severe learning difficulties. In those with severe learning difficulties, digit span, along with other measures of cognitive development, lags behind the level expected on the basis of age. In fact, there is evidence that memory span shows greater impairments in those with severe learning difficulties than other measures included in standard IQ tests (e.g. Baumeister & Bartlett, 1962; Belmont et al., 1967). It has also been found that in those with Down's syndrome, and in others with both mild and severe learning difficulties, there is poor digit span in relation to other language skills as assessed by the Illinois Test of Psycholinguistic Abilities (Bilovsky & Share, 1965; Marinosson, 1974). Down's syndrome children also show poor auditory serial recall performance compared with other memory tasks, such as recognition and visual memory (McDade & Adler, 1980; Marcell & Armstrong, 1982).

These studies have involved comparisons between groups with learning difficulties, at a certain level of mental age (MA), and control groups of normal subjects matched for either mental or chronological age. Such studies establish that subjects with learning difficulties have a deficit in memory span at a given level of mental development. So, for example, Marinosson (1974) found that children with severe learning difficulties at MA 5, had poorer digit span scores, than normal children of the same mental age. This, and similar studies reviewed in Chapter 3, establish that severe learning difficulties are associated with impairments of short-term memory; such studies do not, however, reveal the course of development of memory span in these groups. We know that in Down's syndrome, in particular, where early identification makes longitudinal studies from an early age possible, there is an increasing lag between performance on cognitive tests as chronological age increases (e.g. Carr, 1985). The slower rate of development in these children, compared to normal children, results in their IQ falling as they get older. To put this another way, their mental age increases less rapidly than in normal children.

The following experiments were designed to assess memory span in those with Down's syndrome and others with severe learning difficulties and mental age matched normal children over a wide age range, and to investigate the development of memory span in these groups. The aim was to compare memory span development in normal children with that in people with severe learning difficulties, and also to compare Down's syndrome subjects with a group of other subjects of different aetiology, matched for the severity of their learning difficulties.

In normal development, memory span increases with chronological age, and by definition mental age increases alongside chronological age. In those with learning difficulties, mental age lags behind chronological age. There are a number of possible forms that the relationship between memory development and mental development might take in those with learning difficulties. Previous studies have shown that memory span performance is poor, even in comparison with groups of younger normal children matched for mental age. This could be consistent with a number of different developmental patterns in those with severe learning difficulties. Perhaps the simplest relationship would be that there is a fixed lag between mental age and memory span. Another possibility is that memory span development in those with learning difficulties does not even keep pace with their generally slow rate of mental development. This would result in a severe and increasing deficit in memory span as age increased.

This set of experiments was designed to assess which developmental pattern is true, and to establish whether the pattern of memory span development with age is equivalent in those with Down's syndrome and other people with equally severe learning difficulties.

EXPERIMENT 1

Method

Subjects

These came from two local authority day schools for those with severe learning difficulties. Older subjects were former pupils of these schools now attending local Adult Training Centres. All subjects lived in the community, most with their families but a small number of adults lived in a local hostel; none was institutionalized.

Subjects with severe learning difficulties were divided into two groups: those with Down's Syndrome, and a mixed group. This allows us to establish if deficits in memory span in Down's syndrome subjects are comparable to the deficits in other subjects who have similar intellectual impairments but different aetiologies. The mixed group have a variety of aetiologies: Some have specific clinical syndromes, such as cerebral palsy, others have unspecified brain damage due to accidents or trauma, and the remainder have no specific diagnosis. Although it is difficult to draw conclusions from comparisons of older and younger individuals of different aetiologies, this group can provide a match for intelligence and level of mental development for the Down's syndrome group.

The third group of subjects were normal children whose chronological ages were similar to the mental ages of the groups with severe learning difficulties.

There were 55 subjects in each group: Down's syndrome, severe learning difficulties-mixed aetiology and normal. Details of the chronological ages of the groups are given in Table 4.1.

Materials

As a test of general mental development all subjects were given the English Picture Vocabulary Test (EPVT), a test of vocabulary

TABLE 4.1
Chronological Ages in Years and Months
for Subjects in Experiment 1

	Normal	SLD Down's	SLD Mixed
Median range	6:0	16:2	19:1
Lowest	4:2	9:1	9:9
Highest	8:4	32:0	38:2

N = 55 for each group.

knowledge. This test correlates highly with other measures of verbal intelligence and has been widely used for estimating mental age in people with severe learning difficulties. Digit span was assessed using the auditory sequential memory sub-test from the Illinois Test of Psycholinguistic Ability (ITPA). In this test the lists were read at a fast rate of two digits a second. Starting with a two-digit list, 2 lists at each list length are given until the subject fails to recall a list in correct order. At this point the other lists for this list length and the previous list length are also presented. There are 3 three-digit lists, 4 four-digit lists, 5 five-digit, and 5 six-digit lists in this test.

Procedure

Subjects were tested individually in a separate room at their school or training centre, in a single session lasting between 10 and 15 minutes.

The EPVT raw score was converted into a mental age score using the norm scores from the administrative manual for the test (Brimer & Dunn, 1973). Scoring for the ITPA auditory sequential memory test is two points for each list repeated in correct order on the first attempt, one point for a list correct on the second attempt. Scores relate to the number of correctly repeated lists. As more lists (and therefore longer lists) are correctly recalled, scores increase; higher scores therefore indicate longer memory span.

Results

Details of the mental age and Auditory Sequential Memory scores are given in Table 4.2 for the three groups of subjects. The scores for memory span are the longest list ever correctly repeated.

Correlational Analyses

Normal Children. These children show a range of Auditory Sequential Memory (ASM) scores consistent with the ITPA norms for this range of mental ages (Paraskevopoulos & Kirk, 1969). This group, as expected, show a high correlation between mental age and chronological age: $r = 0.82$, $p < 0.001$, and the range of mental ages in the group is similar to the range of chronological ages. Older children have higher mental ages and they also have higher ASM scores. There were high correlations between chronological age and ASM scores ($r = 0.71$, $p < 0.001$), and between mental age and ASM scores ($r = 0.71$, $p < 0.001$).

TABLE 4.2
Mental Age and Auditory Sequential Memory Scores for
the 3 Groups in Experiment 1

	Mean	Median	Range
Normal children (N = 55)			
MA (years:months)	6:0	6:0	4:4–8:7
ASM score	20.0	20.0	7–34
Actual span	4.0	4.0	3–6
SLD Down's syndrome (N = 55)			
MA (years:months)	5:11	5:10	4:0–8:3
ASM score	10.0	10.0	3–20
Actual span	3.0	3.0	2–4
SLD mixed (N = 55)			
MA (years:months)	6:3	6:6	3:3–9:4
ASM score	15.0	12.0	2–42
Actual span	3.0	3.0	2–7

Note: Actual span = longest list correctly recalled.

Down's Syndrome.   For this group, the increases in ASM scores are less than those for the normal group with a similar range of mental ages. The Down's group ranges in mental age from 4 years to just over 8 years, and there is a significant relationship between mental age and chronological age ($r = 0.44$, $p < 0.01$), although it is not as strong a relationship for this group as it is for normal children ($r = 0.82$). The difference between these two correlation coefficients is statistically significant ($z = 3.53$, $p < 0.001$).

There was no significant correlation between chronological age and ASM scores ($r = 0.14$), but there was a significant correlation between mental age and ASM scores ($r = 0.41$, $p < 0.05$). This correlation, however, is considerably weaker than the equivalent correlation in the normal group ($r = 0.71$). The difference between these correlation coefficients was significant, ($z = 2.22$, $p < 0.001$). There is, therefore, a significantly higher correlation between mental age and ASM scores in normal children, than in those with Down's syndrome having a similar range of mental ages.

Severe Learning Difficulties—Mixed Aetiology.   This group showed a similar pattern to the Down's group, rather than the normal group. There was no significant correlation between mental age and chronological age ($r = 0.17$), and as this is not a homogeneous group one would not necessarily expect one. Also, there was no significant relationship between ASM scores and chronological age ($r = 0.23$), but there was a significant correlation between mental age and ASM scores ($r = 0.43$, $p < 0.01$) very similar to that for mental age and ASM scores in the Down's group ($r = 0.41$); there is no significant difference between these correlation coefficients ($z = 0.09$, N.S.). However, the difference in this relationship between mental age and ASM scores in the mixed aetiology severe learning difficulties group and the normal group was statistically significant ($z = 2.13$, $p < 0.001$). The mixed aetiology severe learning difficulties group show a similar pattern of results to the group of Down's syndrome subjects, rather than the same pattern as the normal children.

These results show that although in normal subjects aged 4 to 8 years there is a substantial correlation between mental age (MA) and memory span, in subjects with severe learning difficulties of equivalent MA, this correlation is much reduced. The subjects with severe learning difficulties, however, are very much older than the normal children of the same MA. It could be, therefore, that this difference in results reflects the different ages of the subjects. In normal subjects, memory span development levels out at an earlier age than the development of vocabulary knowledge that was used here as a measure of MA. If this were also true in those with severe learning difficulties this might provide a possible explanation for the results obtained. If, for many of our subjects with severe learning difficulties, mental development is nearly complete, this might be more nearly true for memory span than for MA as assessed by vocabulary knowledge. This would automatically lead to a lower correlation between MA and ASM in the groups with severe learning difficulties than the normal group.

This position makes a clear prediction: If we look at subjects with severe learning difficulties who are younger we should obtain larger correlations between MA and ASM than we obtained in our complete samples. We tested this prediction by looking separately at the results for subjects who were 16 years old or less. For the Down's syndrome group there were 25 such subjects whose ages ranged from 9:1 to 15:11. The correlation between MA and ASM scores for this group was $r = 0.53$ ($p < 0.01$), which is slightly higher than the correlation for the complete group of $r = 0.41$. The difference between these correlations is, however, small and the value for the younger sub-sample is within 1 standard error of the original value for the sample as a whole. In the severe learning difficulties group of mixed aetiology, there were 22 subjects whose ages ranged from 9:9 to 16:0. In this group, however, the correlation between MA and ASM scores was just $r = 0.25$ (N.S.) which is lower than the equivalent correlation for the complete group of $r = 0.43$. It would seem clear from these results that the low correlation between MA and ASM scores in those with severe learning difficulties obtained in this study does not depend upon having a large proportion of subjects who are mature. The same pattern is true in those with severe learning difficulties who are all 16 years or younger.

These data show differences in the development of memory span between normal subjects and those with severe learning difficulties but they do not tell us about the extent of the deficit in memory span compared to mental age at different stages of intellectual development. That is, whether the deficit is the same at MA 5 as it is at MA 6 or 7. To answer this question it is necessary to examine the absolute size of the memory scores of subjects in each group at different levels of mental development.

EXPERIMENT 2

From each group of subjects seen in Experiment 1 three different mental age groups were selected: low, middle, and high. The groups with severe learning difficulties were chosen from the school groups rather than from the Adult Training Centres so as to avoid too great a range of chronological ages (and level of education). Also, with Down's syndrome subjects there is evidence that deterioration similar to that found in those with Alzheimer's syndrome starts relatively early (Gath, 1981). Subjects were chosen so that groups of Down's and other subjects with severe learning difficulties were individually matched for mental age and chronological age. Three groups of normal children were then selected, again matching mental age scores with the severely subnormal groups. Individual children were only selected if their mental age was within six months of their chronological age, thus avoiding a wide range of intellectual ability in these groups. There were thus nine groups of subjects altogether, with eight subjects in each group. Table 4.3 shows the chronological and mental ages of these matched groups, and the group mean scores for the Auditory Sequential Memory (ASM) test. The data for the ASM test are also illustrated in Fig. 4.1.

Raw scores for the ASM test were subjected to an analysis of variance, with two between-subject variables: types of subject (population); and levels of mental age. This analysis shows that there is a significant difference in ASM scores for the different groups of subjects (normal, Down's syndrome and severe learning difficulties-mixed aetiology): $F(2,63) = 31.224$, $p < 0.001$. There is also a significant effect due to increasing mental age: $F(2,63) = 8.092$, $p < 0.01$ and a highly significant interaction between these two factors: $F(4,63) = 4.935$, $p < 0.002$.

To explore this interaction further a simple main effects analysis was undertaken. The normal children show a significant increase in ASM scores as mental age increases: $(F = 16.14$, $p < 0.05)$. However, there is

TABLE 4.3
Group Means (and Standard Deviations) for Chronological
Ages, Mental Ages (in Years and Months), and Auditory
Sequential Memory for the Subjects in Experiment 2.

	Low	Medium	High
Mental age (EPVT)			
Normal children	5:2 (0.12)	5:9 (0.16)	6:11 (0.31)
Down's Syndrome	5:2 (0.43)	5:9 (0.16)	6:10 (0.39)
SLD mixed	5:2 (0.35)	5:10 (0.16)	6:11 (0.52)
Chronological age			
Normal children	5:2 (0.35)	6:0 (0.53)	6:9 (0.48)
Down's Syndrome	12:6 (2.41)	14:1 (2.81)	17:1 (3.37)
SLD mixed	13:4 (1.57)	14:6 (3.79)	16:5 (2.95)
ASM scores			
MA (EPVT)			
Normal children	13.0 (4.24)	19.8 (2.85)	25.3 (4.32)
Down's Syndrome	9.3 (2.27)	10.8 (4.97)	10.6 (1.32)
SLD mixed	11.1 (2.8)	10.0 (3.5)	13.5 (4.47)
PLA norm	19	21	25

N = 8 for each group

no such change in memory scores for either of the two groups with severe learning difficulties, despite higher mental age scores. For the Down's group, variance between the three mental age levels is very low ($F <$ 1.0), as it is for the mixed aetiology severe learning difficulties group ($F = 1.94$, N. S.). The difference between the normal and severe learning difficulties groups is small at MA 5 years 2 months ($F = 1.82$, N.S.), but as mental age increases so does the difference between normal and severe learning difficulties groups. There is a significant difference between groups at MA 5 years 9 months ($F = 14.11, p < 0.05$) and at MA 6 years 10 months ($F = 26.02, p < 0.01$). There does not appear to be any significant difference between the two severe learning difficulties groups.

EXPERIMENT 3: TWO-YEAR FOLLOW-UP

It appears from the above study that memory span fails to develop at a rate commensurate with increases in mental age in subjects with severe learning difficulties. This conclusion, however, rests on a comparison across different groups of subjects at different stages of development. In order to get more direct evidence on this crucial point we undertook a longitudinal study. By observing changes in memory span in the same

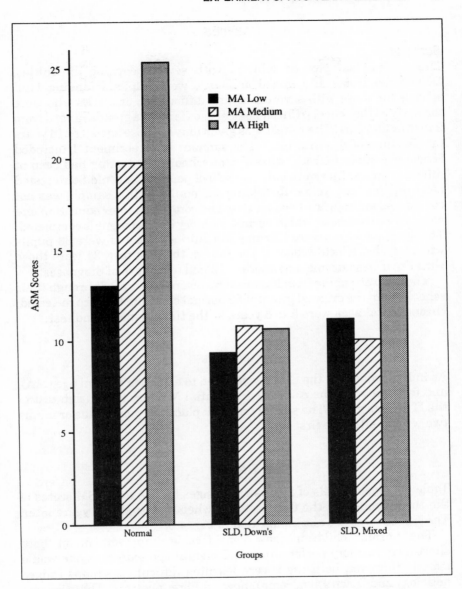

FIG. 4.1. Mean Auditory Sequential Memory scores for subjects in Experiment 2.

individuals across time we can show directly whether development proceeds more slowly in our subjects with severe learning difficulties as compared to controls.

Method

Subjects

The original samples of subjects with severe learning difficulties, Down's syndrome and mixed aetiology, were pupils attending local schools for those with severe learning difficulties, or adults who were formerly at the schools. Chronological ages for these groups ranged from 9 to over 30 years. The re-test was given only to those aged 9 to 16 years (at the time of the first test). The samples in Experiment 1 included school-age subjects from two different schools, but testing had been at different times, therefore only one school population could be re-tested after a gap of two years. Re-testing the adults in this sample was not considered appropriate because they had completed their education and were above the age at which normal memory development is completed. The subjects with severe learning difficulties re-tested were 33 pupils who attended a local school at the time of the first test, 21 were those with Down's syndrome and another 12 had a mixture of diagnoses.

The control sample from Experiment 1 were also traced through their school. From the original group of 55 normal children, 41 were re-tested, chronological ages were 5 to 8 years at the time of the second test.

Procedure

As in Experiment 1, the EPVT was given to establish mental age (MA), and for digit span the Auditory Sequential Memory (ASM) sub-test of the ITPA was given. The second test took place two years (plus or minus two weeks) after the first test.

Results

Table 4.4 gives details of means and ranges for MA and ASM scores of the three groups on the first test and when re-tested two years later. The ASM scores are also illustrated in Fig. 4.2.

The normal children show considerable improvement in both short-term memory performance and mental age scores, as one would expect. However, both the severe learning difficulties groups (mixed aetiology and Down's syndrome) show a different pattern. There is some improvement in mental age, consistent with their slow learning rate, but there does not appear to be any appreciable increase in ASM scores.

Normal Children.   For normal children, increases in mental age are in line with chronological age. The mean MA of the normal children has increased by exactly 24 months. Increases in MA over the two-year

TABLE 4.4

Mental Age and Memory Span Scores on Initial Test and 2-Year Re-test, for Normal, Down's Syndrome, and SLD mixed Groups in Experiment 3

	Mental Age		ASM Score	
	1980	1982	1980	1982
Normal children, N=41 CA (1982) 5:9 to 8:3 years				
Means	5:3	7:3	16.4	22.7
S.D.	(8.5)	(8.4)	(5.1)	(6.5)
Median	5:3	7:3	17.0	21.0
Range	4:1–7:9	5:2–10:3	8–28	13–45
Down's syndrome N=21, CA (1982) 11:1 to 18:7				
Means	5:4	5:10	9.9	10.8
S.D.	(7.7)	(6.2)	(4.0)	(5.4)
Median	5:4	5:11	9.0	11.0
Range	3:11–7:1	4:9–7:3	4–14	4–18
SLD mixed, N=12, CA (1982) 12:5 to 19:1 years				
Means	5:5	5:11	13.3	13.5
S.D.	(10.3)	(10.2)	(8.5)	(7.4)
Median	5:7	6:2	9.5	10.0
Range	3:7–7:3	4:1–7:7	5–32	6–32

period ranged from 11 months to 36 months. ASM scores have also increased over the two-year period for the normal group as a whole. The mean score has increased by just over 6 points. According to the norms for the test given by Paraskevopoulos and Kirk (1969) for the 24 month increase from 5 years 3 months to 7 years 3 months (the mean MA for the group as a whole) the increase in the ASM score would be from 19 to 25 points (a 6 point increase).

Thus, although scores for the group are slightly lower than expected given their MA, the increase in ASM is in line with the increase predicted by the norms for the test. An analysis of variance showed a significant improvement in ASM scores over the two-year period ($F(1,40) = 70.61$, $p < 0.001$) and an equivalent analysis also revealed a significant improvement in MA ($F(1,40) = 518.79, p < 0.001$).

Down's Syndrome.   The mean MA for this group increased by 6 months. An analysis of variance confirmed that this increase in MA for the group over the two-year period was highly significant ($F(1,20) = 34.76, p < 0.001$).

However, changes in ASM scores for the group are minimal and scores are well below the norm scores for the test at this level of MA. The norm scores for the ASM test at age 5.4 and 5.10 (median MAs for the Down's

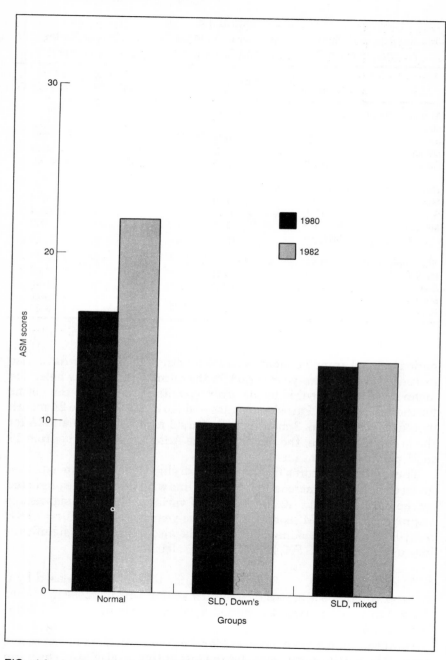

FIG. 4.2. Auditory Sequential Memory scores over a 2-year period.

group in 1980 and 1982) are 19 and 22 points respectively, an increase of 3 points for an increase of 6 months MA. The ASM scores of the Down's syndrome subjects are considerably below this level; they increase less than 1 point over the two-year period. An analysis of variance revealed no significant difference between scores for the first and second test two years later ($F(1,20) = 2.05$, N.S.).

Severe Learning Difficulties—Mixed Aetiology. There were just 12 subjects in this group available for the re-test. The overall mental age scores for this group are similar to those of the Down's syndrome group. The mean increase in MA is 6 months, the same as for the Down's syndrome group. An analysis of variance indicated a significant increase in MA over the two-year period for this group ($F(1,11) = 19.48$, $p < 0.005$).

The mean ASM scores for this group are similar to those of the Down's group, but the range of scores is broader with the mixed group showing higher scores. The means for this mixed aetiology group are between 13 and 14 points on both first and second tests. An analysis of variance confirmed that this minimal increase did not approach significance ($F < 1.0$).

To a large extent the results of this mixed aetiology, severe learning difficulties group are similar to those of the Down's syndrome group. Improvements in mental age are significant and at the level expected given that the group has severe learning difficulties. However, improvements in memory span are small, even considering the level of improvement expected given the modest increases in mental age.

EXPERIMENT 3: FIVE-YEAR FOLLOW-UP

It is possible that two years is too short a time for any development in memory span to be apparent in those with severe learning difficulties. Thus a further test was carried out, with as many subjects as could be traced, five years (plus or minus two weeks) after the original tests.

Method

The EPVT and Auditory Sequential Memory test from ITPA were given to 28 normal children, 10 Down's syndrome, and 8 other subjects with severe learning difficulties, for these subjects there were now three sets of scores: the initial test; re-test after two years; and re-test after five years.

Results

Table 4.5 gives the mean MA and ASM scores for these groups on the three tests. The ASM scores are also illustrated in Fig. 4.3.

The normal children continue to show steady improvement in both ASM scores and MA. In both the groups with severe learning difficulties (Down's syndrome and mixed aetiology) there is steady improvement in MA and also a slight improvement in ASM scores over five years.

Normal Children.   In this group of 28 normal children mental age continues to rise in line with chronological age; the mean MA of the group has increased by 4 years 11 months over five years. The majority of normal children increased their memory span by 2 to 3 items over five years, mean span increasing from 4 items to 6. ASM scores have also increased over five years, mean scores increasing by 12 points (means: 16 and 28). The ASM scores for this group are slightly lower than the norms for their MA given by Paraskevopoulos and Kirk (1969), norm scores are 19 and 33 points (for MA 5:3, 10:2), an increase of 14 points. An analysis of variance showed a significant improvement in ASM scores over five years, $(F(2,54) = 75.3, p < 0.001)$, and a similar analysis of mental age scores also showed significant increases $(F(2,54) = 170.1, p < 0.001)$.

TABLE 4.5

Means (and Standard Deviations) for Mental Age, Auditory Sequential Memory and Digit Span over a Period of 5 Years

	1980	1982	1985
Normal children (N=28)			
Chronological age	4:11 (8.9)	6:11	9:11
Mental age	5:3 (0.91)	7:3 (1.09)	10:2 (2.55)
ASM	16.7 (5.33)	22.4 (6.00)	28.3 (6.97)
Digit span	3.8 (0.61)	4.6 (0.79)	5.5 (0.84)
Down's syndrome (N = 10)			
Chronological age	11:1 (14.8)	13:1	16:1
Mental age	5:1 (0.65)	5:9 (0.60)	6:5 (0.74)
ASM	8.6 (2.41)	10.5 (3.71)	11.7 (4.08)
Digit span	3.1 (0.57)	3.2 (0.42)	3.6 (0.71)
SLD mixed group (N = 8)			
Chronological age	11:0 (12.2)	13:0	16:0
Mental age	5:6 (0.74)	6:2 (0.65)	6:10 (0.66)
ASM	13.1 (7.02)	13.3 (7.07)	16.3 (8.93)
Digit span	3.5 (0.76)	3.5 (0.76)	4.1 (1.13)

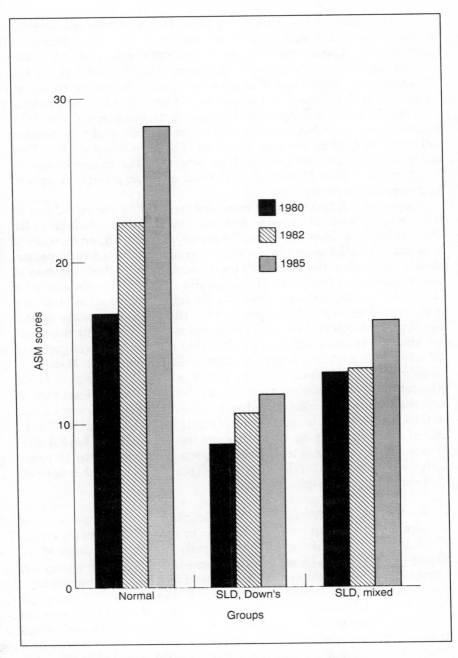

FIG. 4.3. Auditory Sequential Memory scores over a 5-year period.

Down's Syndrome.   This group of 10 Down's syndrome subjects increased mean MA scores by 16 months over five years (increases ranging from 11 to 21 months). An analysis of variance of MA scores showed that improvements were significant ($F(2,18) = 58.7$, $p < 0.01$). ASM scores also show signs of improvement, mean scores increasing by 3 points over five years. Each subject increased scores by 1 to 4 points, with one exception who increased her score by 9 points (she also had the highest increase in MA). An analysis of variance showed a significant difference in ASM scores over five years ($F(2,18) = 9.8$, $p < 0.01$). This analysis does not, however, tell us whether this improvement in Auditory Sequential Memory is at the rate expected given their rate of improvement in Mental Age.

The mean MA for the group increased from 5:1 on the initial test to 6:5 five years later, an increase of 16 months. The ASM norms given for the test for these MAs are 18 and 24 points, respectively, an increase of 6 points. The ASM scores in the Down's group rise from 8 to 11 points, clearly well below the norms for their mental age, and an increase of just 3 points over five years. It was possible, using the norm scores for the test, to compare each individual's actual increase in Auditory Sequential Memory with that predicted by their improvement in mental age. In all cases actual increases were below the expected increase and an analysis of variance showed that this difference was significant ($F(1,9) = 14.5$, $p < 0.01$). It appears that Auditory Sequential Memory is improving in the Down's subjects, but at a very slow rate that is not keeping pace with improvements in mental age. The minimal pace of this change can be appreciated when looking at the actual memory spans of these subjects (the longest string of digits repeated correctly). On the initial test mean span was 3.1 digits and has only increased to 3.6 after five years. On the final test, when subjects were aged 14 to 19 years, only two subjects could reliably recall 4 digits in order, all other subjects still recalling just 3 digits in order.

Severe Learning Difficulties—Mixed Aetiology.   The pattern of results for this group was very similar to that of the Down's group. Overall scores for this group were slightly higher than those of the Down's group, as can be seen in the means in Table 4.5. An analysis of variance comparing the two groups showed that these differences were not significant; there was no difference in MA scores ($F(1,16) = 2.5$, N.S.) or in ASM scores ($F(1,16) = 2.3$, N.S.). Also, there were no significant interactions between the two groups (Down's and severe learning difficulties-mixed) and the level of increase in scores over time, for MA ($F(2,32) = 0.6$, N.S.) and for ASM scores ($F(2,32) = 1.6$, N.S.).

Mental age scores in this group of eight subjects increase at the same rate as the Down's group; the mean increasing by 16 months over five years (range of increases: 9 to 20 months). An analysis of variance showed this increase to be significant ($F(2,14) = 49.5, p < 0.01$).

The mean Auditory Sequential Memory scores increase from 13 to 16 points over five years, individual increases ranged from 1 to 7 points. The mean span increased from 3.5 to 4.1 digits. These means reflect the wider range of memory span performance in this group of subjects with severe learning difficulties, compared with the Down's subjects. On the final test one subject had a span of 6 digits, three had spans of 4 digits, and the remaining four subjects had a memory span of 3 digits. The improvements in ASM scores on the three tests were significant for this group ($F(2,14) = 7.2, p < 0.01$). These improvements in Auditory Sequential Memory, however, were not at the rate predicted by increases in mental age. Mean MAs improved from 5:6 to 6:10 over five years, the ASM norms for these MAs are 20 and 25 points, an increase of 5 points. ASM scores for this group with severe learning difficulties are below the level expected for MA, and the increase in scores is less than expected. An analysis of variance showed a significant difference between subjects' actual increases in Auditory Sequential Memory and those predicted by mental age improvements ($F(1,7) = 5.79, p < .05$).

The results for the Down's syndrome and mixed aetiology severe learning difficulties groups are very similar, with slow, steady improvements in mental age, significant after two years and continuing to improve over five years. Improvements in Auditory Sequential Memory are not significant over two years, but do reach a significant level after five years. However the pace of improvement in Auditory Sequential Memory is very slow, and does not keep up with increases in MA.

GENERAL DISCUSSION

The results of these studies provide a relatively clear picture of the relationship between cognitive development and memory span development in those with severe learning difficulties. The normal children show considerable improvement in both short-term memory performance and mental age scores, as one would expect. However, both groups with severe learning difficulties (mixed aetiology and Down's syndrome) show a different pattern. There is some improvement in mental age, consistent with their slow learning rate, but there does not appear to be any appreciable increase in Auditory Sequential Memory scores. In the first study, digit span in the groups with severe learning difficulties was generally lower than that expected on the basis of their mental ages, and the correlation between mental age and digit span was lower in the groups with severe learning difficulties than in the normal group. When matched groups, who differed in mental age, were compared in Experiment 2, it was shown that digit span failed to increase reliably with mental age in the two groups with severe learning difficulties, unlike in the normal group. This resulted in an increasing lag, between digit span and mental age, in those with severe learning difficulties, as mental age increased.

This marked lack of development of short-term memory in the groups with severe learning difficulties was given even stronger support by the results of the longitudinal study. Although mental age showed reliable increases in the groups with severe learning difficulties in the two-year follow-up there was no reliable increase in digit span over this period. Only over five years was there a reliable increase in digit span scores and here digit span did not improve at the rate expected given the pace of increases in mental age. This contrasted sharply with the pattern in the normal children of reliable increases in both mental age and digit span, which kept pace with each other.

One possible caveat that should be mentioned here is that the comparisons between mental age and digit span development in the present study are based on one measure of ability; the English Picture Vocabulary Test. This is a test of receptive vocabulary knowledge. It could be argued that a different pattern would have emerged with a different measure of mental age. Although this is clearly possible, it does not seem likely. Vocabulary knowledge, as assessed by the EPVT, is a good measure of verbal intelligence. The test results for the normal children are extremely lawful. There is a high correlation between digit span and mental age in this group, and in the longitudinal study, these children show the expected increases in both mental age and digit span. In contrast, in the children with severe learning difficulties, there is little relationship between digit span and mental age. Furthermore, over the five year longitudinal study although these children showed small increases in mental age of the size expected given their learning difficulties, the changes in their digit spans were tiny. Recall that at the end of this study, when aged between 14 and 19 years, only two of the Down's syndrome group could reliably recall four digits in order, all the other subjects in this group could only recall three digits in order. There can be no doubt that short-term memory skills in these children show a profound failure of development, which is poor even in comparison to their slow rate of development of many other intellectual skills.

Overall, there was a striking degree of similarity between the results for the Down's syndrome group and the severe learning difficulties group of mixed aetiology. The pattern of severely retarded short-term memory performance that fails to improve in line with other indices of cognitive development seems to be true of groups with severe learning difficulties in general, rather than to be a specific feature associated with some restricted form of pathology. There have been suggestions of specific auditory memory problems in Down's syndrome (McDade & Adler, 1980; Marcell & Armstrong, 1982) in studies comparing these subjects with normal children, but not including a control group with severe learning difficulties. Our results show that auditory memory deficits may be best described as a common feature of severe learning difficulties rather than a specific problem in Down's syndrome. The one consistent difference which was found between the Down's and severe learning difficulties-mixed aetiology groups, was the much greater variability of digit span in the mixed aetiology group. Severe learning difficulties, including Down's syndrome, appear to be accompanied by short-term memory deficits, but in a relatively small number of cases it is possible to find comparatively well-preserved short-term memory performance.

A major question that is raised by the present findings is how we are to explain the short-term memory deficit found in those with severe learning difficulties. The data presented here are essentially descriptive, but we might hope that an explanation for the deficit in those with severe learning difficulties would make contact with explanations for the development of short-term memory in normal children. In some experiments reviewed in Chapter 3 we explored the factors responsible for the development of memory span in normal children using the effects of word length on serial recall as means of investigating this (Hulme & Tordoff, 1989; Hulme et al, 1984). We found that for normal children the same linear function related recall to speech rate for children of widely different ages. At any given age memory span was roughly constant, as the amount that could be articulated in approximately 1.5 seconds. It was concluded that developmental increases in short-term memory span could be explained in terms of increases in speech rate. Speech rate, in turn, was interpreted as an index of the speed with which material could be rehearsed within an articulatory loop (Baddeley & Hitch, 1974).

We applied the techniques used in those experiments to study the short-term memory system of those with severe learning difficulties. The next chapter describes the relationship between speech rate and the recall of words of different lengths, and the effects of acoustic similarity on memory span, in matched groups of normal children and subjects with severe learning difficulties.

CHAPTER 5

The Articulatory Loop in Severe Learning Difficulties

The studies reported in Chapter 4 clarify the nature of the short-term memory deficits associated with severe learning difficulties. Descriptively, we can say that in severe learning difficulties, whether attributed to Down's syndrome or a variety of other pathologies, verbal short-term memory span shows a marked failure to develop. This failure of development leads to an increasing lag between mental age and short-term memory skill as these children get older. This pattern is quite striking when it is remembered that mental age is, itself, developing at a slow rate in these subjects. It remains to try to specify, in terms of models of memory processes and their development, the origins of this failure of short-term memory development in severe learning difficulties.

In Chapter 3 we argued that by far the most successful explanation for the growth of short-term memory span with age is provided by the idea of an articulatory loop. The articulatory loop holds information in an articulatory form, and is subject to the passive loss of information due to decay. This loss of information can be counteracted by rehearsal, and the rate at which this can be done depends upon the rate at which items can be articulated. Our own studies have shown that this general framework gives a close, quantitative, explanation for developmental increases in short-term memory span with age. These experiments have involved relating recall of sequences of words of different spoken lengths to the rate at which these words can be articulated (Hulme & Tordoff, 1989; Hulme et al., 1984). In groups of normal children of different ages, and adults, it was found that the same linear function related recall to speech rate. At any given age memory span was constant, as the amount that could be articulated in approximately 1.5 seconds. It was concluded that developmental increases in short-term memory span could be explained in terms of increases in speech rate. Speech rate in turn was interpreted as an index of the speed with which material could be rehearsed within the articulatory loop.

An important question that arises from this work is whether the short-term memory problems of those with severe learning difficulties can be explained in terms of slow speech rate. This seems a strong possibility, particularly for Down's syndrome subjects. As described in Chapter 1, Down's syndrome subjects experience a variety of speech and language difficulties. In particular, their speech is often described as slurred and slow (e.g. Gibson, 1978); these difficulties, may, in turn, relate to structural abnormalities of their vocal tract, and more general problems in planning and executing complex motor sequences such as those involved in speaking. In this respect they may be comparable to the dysarthric children studied by Raine et al. (1991) whose slow rate of speech was found to be related to their severe short-term memory difficulties.

The first experiment applies the techniques used in our earlier experiments with normal children (Hulme & Tordoff, 1989; Hulme et al., 1984) to explore these issues, by relating recall of words of different lengths to the rate at which they can be articulated in Down's syndrome subjects and others with severe learning difficulties.

EXPERIMENT 1

The effects of variations in word length on serial recall were examined in a group with Down's syndrome, a group with severe learning difficulties of mixed aetiology, and normal children. These groups were matched for mental age, so the normal children were at the same level of mental development as the subjects with severe learning difficulties. In order to discover any developmental changes in performance, three mental age groups were included.

Method

Subjects

There were three mental age groups (with mean mental ages: 5:2, 5:9, 6:11) for each of the three groups of subjects: Down's syndrome, severe learning difficulties-mixed aetiology, and normal children. There were thus nine groups of subjects, with eight subjects in each group. These were the same subjects as had participated in Experiment 2, in Chapter 4.

Materials
In order to be able to relate recall to speech rate, measures of both variables were obtained from three pools of words: words of short spoken duration (one syllable words); of medium spoken duration (two syllable words); and of long spoken duration (three syllable words). Five words of each length were chosen from Edwards' (1978) list of high-frequency words in children's reading books. The short words were: bus, car, fish, pig, tree. The medium words were: apple, lady, monkey, tiger, water. The long words were: banana, elephant, fire-engine, kangaroo, policeman. These pools of words were used to construct lists of 3, 4, and 5 words by sampling at random without replacement. There were 5 lists for each word length (short, medium, long) and for each list length (3, 4, and 5 words). The list length presented to each subject was chosen on the basis of their digit span to avoid "floor" and "ceiling" effects. The majority of subjects with severe learning difficulties (in both the Down's and mixed groups) had spans of three digits. Their serial recall ability, therefore, was tested on lists of 3 words. In each of the groups with severe learning difficulties (Down's and mixed) matched at mental age (MA) 6:11 there were two subjects with spans of four digits, these subjects were tested with lists of 4 words. For the normal children, the younger children had digit spans of three, but those in the higher MA groups had spans of four and five digits.

Procedure

Each of the subjects was tested individually, in a quiet room near their classroom. Testing was spread over three days, so that each test session could be kept short. Each of the three test sessions included testing of serial recall and speech rate for one word length, and would last between 10 and 15 minutes (including a short break between testing serial recall and recording speech rate). The order in which the three word lengths were presented to individuals was varied randomly within all groups.

In the first test session the experimenter took care to establish that the subject understood the serial recall task. The experimenter started by giving the subject lists of 3 digits, and encouraging the subject to repeat the sequence. To check whether subjects understood that the sequence should be recalled in order the experimenter would say 3 numbers, repeat them in a different order and ask the child whether the two lists were the "same" or "different".

The subject was then asked to repeat the individual words to be used to test recall, this served to check that the subject had no difficulty in saying the words, followed by up to three practice trials on the serial recall task. The subject was then given the test lists. Each list was read at a rate of one word a second. Immediately after hearing the list the subject responded by repeating it. Credit was only given for recall of words in their correct serial position.

After these lists the speech rate samples were obtained. Pairs of words of the appropriate word length were presented and the subject would repeat the two words as fast as possible. Each subject was given three pairs of words to repeat five times in all. Some subjects in the groups with severe learning difficulties found this task very difficult, and could not always manage five repetitions of two words without long pauses. In these cases they were also recorded repeating single words. Previous research has shown these procedures give equivalent results (Hulme et al., 1984). The times obtained were transformed into speech rates, in words per second, and averaged for each word length.

Results

The results are shown in Figs 5.1, 5.2, and 5.3 for each mental age where the mean number recalled per list is plotted as a function of speech rate for each word length and for each subject group. Thus, each group contributes three points to these graphs: a point for short words (highest speech rate and highest recall for that group); a point for medium length words (lower speech rate and lower recall); and a point for long words (lowest speech rate and lowest recall).

The recall and speech rate scores plotted in Figs 5.1–5.3 were subjected to analysis of variance.

Serial Recall

A split-plot analysis of variance was performed on the mean number of words recalled in correct serial position on each list, in which the factors were subject type (normal, severe learning difficulties-Down's, severe learning difficulties-mixed), mental age (low, medium, high) and word length. This revealed a significant effect of word length ($F(2,126) = 76.96, p < 0.001$) a significant effect of subject type ($F(2,63) = 6.06, p < 0.005$) and a significant interaction between these two factors ($F(4,126) = 11.59, p < 0.001$). This interaction was explored further by a simple main effects analysis. This revealed that although recall of the different word lengths differed reliably in the normal group ($F = 18.65, p < 0.01$), there was no significant effect of word length in either the Down's group ($F = 2.68$, N.S.) or the group with severe learning difficulties of mixed aetiology ($F = 1.53$, N.S.). The different groups showed reliable differences in recall for the short words ($F = 39.01, p < 0.001$) and

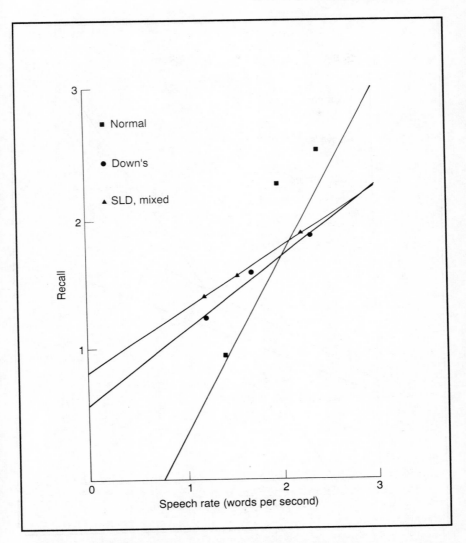

FIG. 5.1. Relationship between word length, speech rate, and serial recall for subjects of mental age 5:2.

medium words ($F = 19.19$, $p < 0.05$) but there was no reliable difference in recall between groups for the long words ($F < 1.0$).

The main effect of subject type was further explored using a Tukey HSD test. This revealed a significant difference in recall between the normal and Down's syndrome groups ($p < 0.01$) and also between the normal and mixed aetiology-severe learning difficulties group ($p < 0.05$).

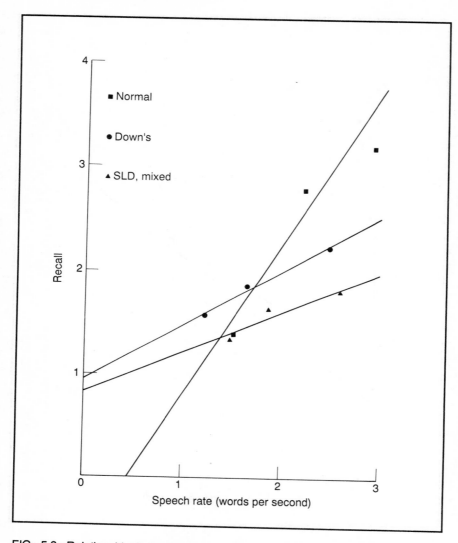

FIG. 5.2. Relationship between word length, speech rate, and serial recall for subjects of mental age 5:9.

There was no reliable difference between recall for the two groups with severe learning difficulties, however.

Speech Rate
The same analysis was performed on the speech rate scores. This revealed a main effect of subject type $(F(2,63) = 4.56, p < 0.02)$ and a

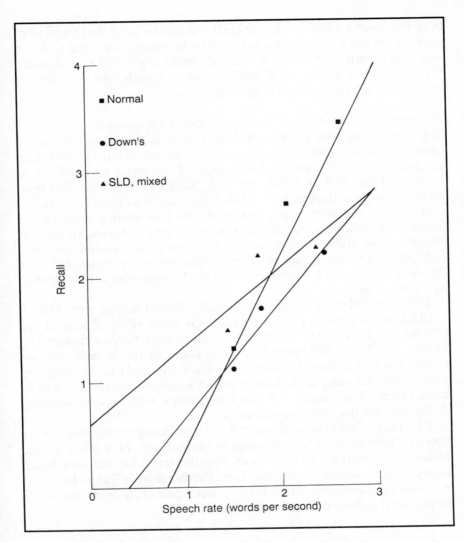

FIG. 5.3. Relationship between word length, speech rate, and serial recall for subjects of mental age 6:11.

main effect of word length ($F(2,126) = 342.54, p < 0.001$). No other factors or interactions were significant.

This analysis shows that for all groups there were reliable differences in speech rate for the short, medium, and long words. A Tukey HSD test revealed that the short words were spoken more quickly than the medium ($p = 0.01$) and the medium words were spoken more quickly than the long ($p < 0.01$). A Tukey HSD test also showed that there were reliable differences in speed of articulation between the normal children and both groups with severe learning difficulties ($p < 0.05$ in each case). However, there was no reliable difference in speech rate between the two groups with severe learning difficulties.

Relationship between Serial Recall and Speech Rate Scores
In previous research, with normal children of different ages, the same linear function relating recall to speech rate has always provided an adequate fit to the scores for groups of different ages (Hitch & Halliday 1983; Hulme & Tordoff, 1989; Hulme et al., 1984; Nicolson, 1981). It is clear that in Figs 5.1–5.3 the functions relating recall to speech rate are very much flatter in the two groups with severe learning difficulties, than in the case of normal children. To test the reliability of this, regression functions were calculated for each individual and the slope estimates obtained were compared in a two-way analysis of variance in which the factors were subject groups and mental age.

This revealed a highly significant main effect of subject type ($F(2,63) = 12.63$, $p < 0.001$) and a marginally significant effect of mental age ($F(2,63) = 3.22$, $p < 0.05$). Both these effects were further explored by means of a Tukey HSD test. The mean slope for the normal children (1.65s) was higher than that for the Down's (0.69s) and that for the group with severe learning difficulties of mixed aetiology (0.54s) ($p < 0.01$ in both cases). The slopes for the two groups with severe learning difficulties did not differ significantly.

The main effect of mental age reflects a tendency for the slope of the function to increase with increases in mental age. This effect should probably be treated with caution as a similar trend has not been found in previous studies of normal children. Furthermore, a Tukey HSD test revealed no significant differences between paired comparisons of the slopes for the three different mental ages.

Discussion

The results of this experiment reveal very clear differences between the effects of word duration on serial recall in normal children and children with severe learning difficulties of different aetiologies and at a range of different mental ages.

Let us consider the results of the normal children first. The results obtained here are very similar to those obtained in our previous research with normal children (Hulme et al., 1984). The slope of the function relating recall to speech rate for the normal children here (1.65s) is virtually identical to the slope of 1.5s fitting the results of normal children from age 4 years upwards and adults in our previous study.

This result can be interpreted in terms of the concept of the articulatory loop of Baddeley and Hitch's (1974) working memory model. This is a store which codes information in an articulatory form, and which is susceptible to spontaneous decay. Information is preserved in the store by means of a process of rehearsal that consists of activating articulatory programs for the items in the store. Word length affects the time it takes to execute such programs and so slows the rate at which items can be rehearsed; because the store is limited in terms of time fewer long words can be rehearsed within the decay time of the store than short words.

Speech rate is seen as a measure of rehearsal rate in this system. The natural interpretation of the results for normal children presented here, and in our previous studies (Hulme & Tordoff, 1989; Hulme et al., 1984), is that the capacity of this store does not change with age, but instead changes in short-term memory performance simply reflect changes in the rate of rehearsal of information in the store. Put another way, the amount of material that can be remembered at any given age is actually constant when expressed in terms of the time taken to articulate that information. This constant can be measured in terms of the slope of the linear function relating recall to speech rate and appears to be roughly 1.5 seconds worth of speech for adults and children (Baddeley et al., 1975; Hulme et al., 1984).

It is interesting that the very consistent relationship between recall and speech rate found in normal subjects of widely differing ages has been shown to break down in the groups with severe learning difficulties studied here. Although the groups with severe learning difficulties articulate the words of differing lengths at reliably different rates, as do normal children, their recall is not reliably affected by word length. This results in the very much flatter function relating recall to speech rate in these groups.

There would seem to be two ways of explaining this pattern in terms of the articulatory loop. One possibility is simply to argue that the capacity of this loop is much smaller in the subjects with severe learning difficulties than in normal children. There is, however, a more radical proposal which seems to fit the details of the data better. This is to suggest that the flattening of the speech rate recall function in those with severe learning difficulties reflects the absence of rehearsal in these subjects. Because of this, those with severe learning difficulties are really failing to utilize the articulatory loop efficiently. This fits in with the results reported in the previous chapter that there is a marked failure of memory span development in those with severe learning difficulties as mental age increases. We have shown that in normal children the development of memory span with age follows increases in speech rate closely. The absence of any reliable effect of word length in those with severe learning difficulties, coupled with the profound lack of development in short-term memory in these groups would be a natural consequence of a failure of rehearsal.

EXPERIMENT 2

The other major demonstration of speech coding in short-term memory apart from the effect of word length, is the detrimental effect of acoustic similarity on serial recall (Baddeley, 1966; Conrad, 1964; Conrad & Hull, 1964). It has been shown that the size of this effect, unlike the effect of word length, varies with age, having progressively more effect on recall between the age of 4 and 10 years (Hulme, 1984). In a further study this change in the size of the acoustic-similarity effect with age has been shown to be closely related to changes in speech rate, and, by inference, rehearsal rate, with age (Hulme & Tordoff, 1989). In view of the close relationship between the effects of acoustic similarity and word length on serial recall, it becomes important to know what effect acoustic similarity has on serial recall in those with severe learning difficulties. This was explored in the present experiment.

Method

A memory span procedure was used to test memory for acoustically similar and dissimilar words.

Subjects
The subjects were the same as in Experiment 1.

Materials
The words used were the names of the pictures used by Conrad (1971). There was a set of eight acoustically similar words (rat, cat, mat, hat, bat, man, bag, tap) and eight acoustically dissimilar words (girl, bus, train, spoon, fish, horse, clock, hand). These words are the same as used in our previous studies of the effects of acoustic similarity on serial recall in children (Hulme, 1984; Hulme & Tordoff, 1989). A set of word lists was constructed by randomly selecting from each of the word pools without replacement. For each type of word, four sequences were constructed for each sequence length from two to seven words.

Procedure

General procedural details were the same as in Experiment 1. Memory span for each type of word list was determined by presenting lists of increasing length. Testing began for all children with the two word sequences. The memory span for each type of list was determined as the longest sequence that the child managed to repeat in correct serial order without error, plus 0.25 for each correct longer list.

Presentation of the acoustically-similar and dissimilar lists was blocked: Half the children in each group began with the similar lists, and half with the dissimilar lists. Once the child failed on three out of four lists of a given type and a given length no further presentations of that type of list were given.

Results

The means and standard deviations of the memory span scores for all groups are shown in Table 5.1.

These scores were subjected to a split-plot analysis of variance in which the factors were subject group (normal, severe learning difficulties-Down's, severe learning difficulties-mixed) mental age, and list type. This revealed a significant main effect of subject group ($F(2,63) = 57.06$, $p < 0.001$) of mental age ($F(2,63) = 10.35$, $p < 0.001$) and of list type ($F(1,63) = 112.6$, $p < 0.001$). There were also two significant interactions. These were between subject group and list-type ($F(2,63) = 15.0$, $p < 0.001$) and between subject group and mental age ($F(4,63) = 4.62$, $p < 0.025$). Both of these interactions were further explored by means of simple main effects analyses.

TABLE 5.1

Means (and Standard Deviations) for Memory Span Scores for Acoustically Similar (AS) and Acoustically Dissimilar (AD) Lists for the 3 Groups in Experiment 2 as a Function of Mental Age

Mental Age	Normal Children		SLD, Down's		SLD, Mixed	
	AS	AD	AS	AD	AS	AD
5.2	2.58	3.28	2.33	2.6	2.33	2.58
	(0.08)	(0.50)	(0.09)	(0.13)	(0.18)	(0.15)
5.9	2.9	3.7	2.4	2.63	2.28	2.38
	(0.13)	(0.13)	(0.09)	(0.09)	(0.12)	(0.13)
6.11	3.35	4.33	2.5	2.9	2.33	2.7
	(0.13)	(0.21)	(0.13)	(0.13)	(0.09)	(0.16)

The interaction between subject group and list type clearly reflects the lesser sensitivity of the groups with severe learning difficulties to acoustic similarity. Simple main effects analyses revealed that in the normal children there is a significant difference in span for the acoustically similar and dissimilar lists (F (2,63) = 117.6, $p < 0.01$). For the Down's group this difference is also significant although it is smaller (F (2,63) = 15.6, $p < 0.01$), as it is for the group with severe learning difficulties of mixed aetiology (F (2,63) = 19.1, $p < 0.01$). The difference between subject groups in recall of the dissimilar words (F (1,126) = 71.6, $p < 0.01$) is larger than the difference for the similar lists (F (1,126) = 21.9, $p < 0.01$).

The interaction between subject groups and mental age reflects the fact that memory span improves more with mental age in the normal children than in either group with severe learning difficulties. Memory span shows significant increases with mental age in the normal children (F (2,63) = 17.61, $p < 0.01$) but not in the Down's (F (2,63) = 1.2, N.S.) or in the mixed aetiology group with severe learning difficulties ($F < 1.0$).

Discussion

There are clear differences in the effects of acoustic similarity on memory span in normal children compared to the subjects with severe learning difficulties. In the normal children recall shows steady increases as mental age and chronological age increase, and acoustic similarity has a detrimental effect on recall. Both groups with severe learning difficulties show a pattern of performance which is different to that in the normal group; recall does not reliably improve with increasing mental age, and the effect of acoustic similarity on memory span is smaller.

In the case of normal children, it was argued in Chapter 2 that an increase in the size of the acoustic-similarity effect with age is a consequence of changes in speech rate with age. The argument here is that both the effect of acoustic similarity and the effect of word length reflect the operation of the articulatory loop of Baddeley and Hitch's (1974) working memory model. This is a store which codes information in terms of articulatory or speech motor programs. The store is susceptible to loss of information over time due to decay. However, loss of information can be prevented by a process of rehearsal which consists of the cyclic reactivation of speech motor programs. The word-length effect is attributable to the fact that long words are represented by speech motor programs of long temporal duration, and fewer such programs can be rehearsed or executed within the decay time of the store, than is the case for short words. Acoustic similarity, on the other hand, affects the relative discriminability of items within this store. Acoustically similar items have similar articulatory traces, which means that any loss of information due to decay affects them more adversely than acoustically dissimilar items. It is proposed that this loss of discriminability results in errors occurring during the rehearsal process; such errors arise from guessing based on the available partial cues concerning an item. This provides an explanation for why changes in the magnitude of the acoustic-similarity effect with age correlate highly with changes in speech rate with age (see Hulme & Tordoff, 1989). The more frequently items are rehearsed, the higher is the probability that an error may be introduced during rehearsal.

Both groups with severe learning difficulties show less sensitivity to acoustic similarity even in the highest mental age group. It was argued earlier that both the effects of acoustic similarity and word length reflect a process of rehearsal of articulatory codes within short-term memory. The attenuation of the acoustic-similarity effect in those with severe learning difficulties, coupled with the previous demonstration of a very small effect of word length in these groups, can be taken as further evidence for an impairment of this rehearsal process in these groups.

GENERAL DISCUSSION

The present experiments have clarified the nature of the short-term memory deficit in those with severe learning difficulties. In these experiments, the performance of subjects with Down's syndrome and subjects with severe learning difficulties of other aetiologies have been remarkably similar, but quite different to the performance of normal children.

In normal children there is a close link between the rate at which material is articulated and how well it is recalled, such that in a serial recall task children of all ages recall as much as they can say in about 1.5 seconds (Hulme et al., 1984). The large increases in memory span with age in normal development are well predicted by corresponding increases in speech rate, which may be viewed as an index of the maximum speed of rehearsal in short-term memory. It is important to emphasize that rehearsal speed is seen here as a structural limitation, not a change in the strategic use of rehearsal, which does not provide a satisfactory explanation of developmental increases in memory span (see Chapter 3).

In contrast to this pattern of performance in normal children, Experiment 1 showed that there is a severe flattening of the function relating recall to speech rate in Down's syndrome and other subjects with severe learning difficulties. This was interpreted in terms of an absence of rehearsal in these subjects and this view was further strengthened by the finding of an attenuated acoustic-similarity effect in these same groups in Experiment 2. It should be noted that the presence of an acoustic-similarity effect, although in an attenuated form, is consistent with a failure to rehearse following the explanation for the acoustic- similarity effect advanced in Chapter 3. Once items are encoded into the articulatory loop, acoustic similarity will serve to impair the discriminability of memory traces for these items. Rehearsal, in this view, simply serves to increase the size of the effect because misidentification of items occurs.

There may appear to be a contradiction here, in that if the acoustic-similarity effect is related to rehearsal, and subjects with severe learning difficulties fail to rehearse we might expect them not to be affected by acoustic similarity. Clearly it is necessary for us to postulate that even in the absence of rehearsal there is the opportunity for misidentifications of acoustically similar traces to occur. The question is when do such misidentifications occur? We would argue that they occur when the decaying traces of items are retrieved from the articulatory loop during recall. We have, at the moment, no explicit theory of the processes whereby information in the articulatory loop is retrieved during recall. In our view, it is a reasonable assumption, however, that the process of retrieval during recall is the same as the process that allows the re-identification of items during rehearsal. This idea will be discussed a little further in the last Chapter (see also Hulme et al., 1991).

The lack of rehearsal also provides a natural explanation for the failure of memory span to develop in children with severe learning difficulties. On the basis of the experiments described in Chapter 3, relating changes in memory span to speech rate, it has been argued that a sufficient explanation for the improvements in memory span observed is in terms of increases in speech rate, and hence rehearsal rate, with age (Hulme et al., 1984). Now, if those with severe learning difficulties fail to utilize rehearsal to maintain information in this store, even though their articulatory skills may improve with age, there is no reason on this view for any change in span to take place.

The idea of a rehearsal deficit in people with learning difficulties has a long history. Most of the studies of this question differ in at least two important ways from the present studies, however. Typically, subjects in these studies have had moderate, rather than severe learning difficulties, and material has been presented visually rather than auditorily, as in the present experiments. For example, in the classic study by Belmont and Butterfield (1969) subjects were able to set the pace of item presentation. Normal children left gaps between items with particularly long gaps after three items. This was considered to be evidence for rehearsal in groups of three. Subjects with moderate learning difficulties, on the other hand, did not show this pattern, preferring fast presentation throughout the sequence. In a subsequent study (Belmont & Butterfield, 1971), rehearsal training improved performance in subjects with moderate learning difficulties to the level of the mental age matched control children.

The link between these findings and the present experiments is not particularly direct. Probably the most important difference is modality of presentation. It is possible that children start to rehearse visual material at a later age than auditory material (e.g. Hitch & Halliday, 1983) and the most natural explanation for recent findings relating recall to speech rate is that normal children as young as 4 years old spontaneously rehearse auditory material (Hulme et al., 1984). A failure to rehearse visually presented material in subjects with moderate learning difficulties would not necessitate the view that the source of the auditory memory span deficit in those with severe learning difficulties was a rehearsal deficit.

The question of comparability between people with moderate and severe learning difficulties is also important. The present study has focused on the cognitive mechanisms responsible for the memory impairments in those with severe learning difficulties. The simplest assumption would be that the memory impairments of people with moderate and severe learning difficulties fall on a continuum, varying only in severity. One recent study, however, calls this idea into question. Das (1985) found a relationship between reading time and memory span for digits in people with moderate learning difficulties. He interpreted this in terms of speed of item identification being an important determinant of recall in the mildly subnormal. This follows the ideas developed by Case, Kurland, and Goldberg (1982) in studies of normal memory span development. This interpretation is almost certainly wrong, however, as reading time confounds the time taken to identify items with the time taken to articulate them. When the contribution of recognition processes are minimized, measures of articulation rate remain good predictors of recall in normal children (Hulme et al., 1984). Furthermore, measures of identification speed do not provide an adequate explanation for the differences in recall between words of different lengths, whereas differences in articulation rate do (Hitch et al., 1989). These findings show that the crucial determinant of recall is articulation speed rather than item identification speed. Das's results do suggest, however, that in people with moderate learning difficulties measures of articulation rate relate quite closely to recall. This contrasts sharply with the present findings that those with severe learning difficulties show a negligible relationship between speech rate and recall.

A direct test of the present proposal, that the short-term memory deficits of those with severe learning difficulties arise from a failure to rehearse, would be to carry out a training study using auditorily presented material. If an important source of the memory span deficit in those with severe learning difficulties is a failure to rehearse, then, providing such training is successful, it should improve memory span and also increase the sensitivity of such subjects to manipulations of acoustic similarity and word length in serial recall. Theoretically, such a result would provide crucial support for the present explanation of the memory deficit seen in people with severe learning difficulties and provide further evidence relevant to theories of short-term memory and its development. We present a study of this issue in the next chapter.

CHAPTER 6

Improving Memory Span in Severe Learning Difficulties

The results from the experiments reported in Chapters 4 and 5 seem to be well explained in terms of the concept of an articulatory loop (Baddeley & Hitch, 1974). Normal children show increases in memory span with age that are closely related to corresponding developmental increases in speech rate. Speech rate is seen as an index of the speed with which information can be rehearsed within the articulatory loop. In normal children of different ages there is a close quantitative relationship between how quickly words can be spoken and how well they are recalled. This relationship is particularly important because it offers an explanation for differences between both materials and subjects of different ages. Indeed, even within an age group, differences in speech rate correlate quite well with individual differences in memory span (e.g. Baddeley et al., 1975; Standing et al., 1980).

In contrast to this picture in normal development, in those with severe learning difficulties there are impairments in short-term memory skills that point to a deficit in the use of rehearsal within the articulatory loop. In these subjects there are changes in speech rate with age but there is a failure of memory span to show commensurate development (Chapter 4). In addition, these subjects are much less sensitive to the effects of both word length and acoustic similarity on serial recall than are younger normal children of the same mental age (Chapter 5). All of these results are consistent with the idea that people with severe learning difficulties fail to benefit from rehearsing material within the articulatory loop. If they did so, their memory spans would improve as their speech rate increased with age, and they would be more sensitive to the effects of word length and acoustic similarity.

This view leads naturally to the prediction that if subjects with severe learning difficulties could be induced to rehearse by training they should increase their memory spans. They should also show increased sensitivity to markers for the effects of rehearsal, such as the acoustic-similarity and word-length effects. Such a result would have practical implications for improving short-term memory skills in people with severe learning difficulties. Theoretically, it would provide crucial support for the present explanation of the memory deficit seen in people with severe learning difficulties and provide further evidence relevant to theories of short-term memory and its development. In this chapter we present a study that tests this idea, by examining the effects of rehearsal training on digit span and the acoustic-similarity effect in people with severe learning difficulties. Before going on to present this study, however, we need first to consider, briefly, previous work concerned with rehearsal deficits in learning difficulties.

As noted in Chapter 5, the idea that people with learning difficulties are impaired in their use of rehearsal is not new, although the evidence used to support this view has been of a different sort to that presented in this book. Some of the previous evidence was briefly discussed in Chapter 3, where it was pointed out that studies of this issue have invariably involved memory for visually presented material with children who have only moderate, rather than severe, learning difficulties. As we argued earlier, it is reasonable to suppose that the short-term memory difficulties seen in moderate and severe learning difficulties merely differ along a dimension of severity. This is an assumption, however, and has not yet been adequately tested.

Within the research tradition dealing with memory for visually presented materials in children with moderate learning difficulties, there have also been many attempts to improve short-term memory skills by training rehearsal. Because of the differences between these studies and the present study, we will not go into much detail here, a number of reviews are available elsewhere (Campione & Brown, 1977; N. R. Ellis, 1979; Kail, 1990).

The general results of rehearsal training are impressive. Belmont and Butterfield (1971), as described in Chapter 3, were able to improve recall in their subjects with moderate learning difficulties to match the level of age-matched normal control subjects. Similar results were also obtained by Brown, Campione, Bray, and Wilcox (1973). It has also been possible to find impressive evidence of the durability of rehearsal training. Brown et al. (1974) showed that the effects of training lasted for six months, although later studies have shown that such durability depends upon over-learning and extensive practice in the initial training phase (Borkowski & Cavanagh, 1979). It also appears that such training is highly task-specific; Brown et al. (1974) found that switching from a serial recall task, to a probed recall task, resulted in their trained group of subjects being reduced to the level of their untrained group.

In summary, it is well established that for subjects with less severe learning difficulties than those studied in our own experiments, rehearsal training can have considerable beneficial effects on short-term memory performance. It therefore seemed reasonable to hope that rehearsal training could have beneficial effects on the short-term memory skills of subjects with severe learning difficulties. In the next experiment it was decided to look directly at the possibility of training short-term memory rehearsal strategies in people with severe learning difficulties. We decided to look at the effects of acoustic similarity as a marker for the use of rehearsal. To the extent that rehearsal training is effective in increasing the use of articulatory rehearsal, it was predicted that memory span should increase, and that the size of the difference in recall between acoustically similar and dissimilar lists should also increase. These predictions follow directly from our studies concerning the mechanisms responsible for the acoustic-similarity effect in normal children, and its development with age, described in Chapter 3.

REHEARSAL TRAINING AND THE ACCOUSTIC SIMILARITY EFFECT
Method

Design
Memory span for digits and acoustically similar and dissimilar words was assessed before and after rehearsal training in a group of adolescents with severe learning difficulties. The changes produced by rehearsal training were compared with the performance of two control groups. An untrained, but repeatedly tested, control group provided a means of checking that any effects of training were specific to rehearsal training and not simply attributable to repeated testing. A second, unseen control group were simply tested at the beginning and end of the experiment. This group provides a true baseline against which to compare any changes seen in the rehearsal trained and repeatedly tested groups.

Digit span was assessed in all subjects at the beginning and end of the experiment to provide a check on the extent to which any effects were specific to the materials on which subjects had been trained.

Subjects

A total of 24 adolescents with severe learning difficulties participated in this experiment. They all came from the same school and were divided into three groups of eight subjects. In the trained group there were four males and four females with a mean age of 16 years 8 months (range 13:11 to 17:11). The repeatedly tested control group comprised two males and six females whose mean age was once again 16 years 8 months (range 14:2 to 19:0). The unseen control group consisted of four males and four females whose mean age was 16 years 11 months (range 13:11 to 18:9).

An estimate of mental age was obtained for all subjects by using four sub-tests of the WISC-R: Vocabulary, Similarities, Block Design, and Object Assembly. The average estimated mental age for the rehearsal trained group was 7:9; for the repeatedly tested control group was 7:5; and for the unseen control group was 7:11.

Materials

Digit Span: Eight lists of random digits were constructed at each successive list length from 2 to 7. This gave two parallel forms of a digit span test each consisting of four lists at each list length. This allowed digit span measures to be based on the average of two determinations for greater reliability.

Acoustic Similarity: Eight random word lists were constructed at each successive list length from 2 to 7. The acoustically similar lists were composed of words drawn from the same pool of eight items used previously (rat, bat, cat, mat, hat, bag, man, tap) as were the eight items in the dissimilar pool (hand, girl, clock, fish, train, horse, spoon, bus). Once again this gave two parallel forms of a memory span test consisting of four lists of similar and dissimilar words at each list length.

Procedure

General procedural details were the same as in earlier experiments. Practice trials were given at the start of each memory span test to ensure that subjects understood the nature of the serial recall task. Memory spans for digits and words were measured in separate sessions. Memory span for each type of word list was determined by presenting lists of increasing length. Testing began for all subjects with the two-word sequences and was discontinued when the subject made three errors in a block of four trials at a given list length. A second determination of span for these materials was then made by going back to start re-testing on the list length at which the subject had performed perfectly, testing again discontinued when an error occurred on three out of four lists of a given length. Order of conditions was randomized in each group.

Rehearsal Training

Trained Group: Each subject was given a course of rehearsal training which consisted of one daily session of approximately 10 minutes duration over a period of 10 days. These training sessions occurred daily from Monday to Friday in two consecutive weeks at the school. Testing of memory span occurred at the end of the week prior to commencement of training and at the beginning of the week after training was completed.

During the training sessions the experimenter trained the subjects to use an overt cumulative rehearsal strategy, based upon the method developed by Brown, Campione, and Murphy (1974). Materials for the rehearsal training consisted of randomly constructed lists of similar and dissimilar words of increasing lengths. In this technique the subject repeats successively longer sequences as each individual word is spoken by the experimenter (E-hand, S-hand; E-fish, S-hand, fish; E-clock, S-hand, fish, clock; and so on). In combination with this strategy a "fast finish" system was employed whereby cumulative rehearsal was employed for all but the final item: The latter acting as a cue for immediate recall of the whole list. Each training session continued until the subject was visibly failing to concentrate on the task or until they failed six times at a given span length using the strategy. Training in this manner was given for both acoustically similar and dissimilar lists.

Repeatedly Tested Control Group: These subjects, like the trained group, were seen for 10 minute sessions over 10 days. In these sessions, however, no training in rehearsal was given. Instead, the subjects were simply given word sequences of increasing lengths to recall using the same materials as used in the rehearsal training. This therefore equates the amount of experience in performing a memory span task between the two groups.

Unseen Control Group: These subjects were simply tested for their memory span for the acoustically similar and dissimilar words and digits at the beginning and end of the study.

Results

Scoring: Memory span for each type of list was determined as the longest sequence that the subject managed to repeat without error plus a score of 0.25 for each longer list that was correctly recalled. Span for digits, and for similar and dissimilar words was determined twice on each occasion (twice before and twice after the two school weeks of training) and an average of these two scores taken as the memory span for that type of material.

Acoustic Similarity: The average spans for the acoustically similar and dissimilar words on each test are shown in Table 6.1.

For the scores on the acoustically similar and dissimilar lists there appears to be a general improvement for both the Rehearsal Training and Repeatedly Tested Groups across the two times of testing. There is a suggestion that recall of the dissimilar lists has benefited more from rehearsal training than recall of the similar lists, although this effect is small.

The memory span scores for similar and dissimilar words were entered into a three-way analysis of variance in which the factors were Group, Acoustic Similarity, and Time of Testing. This revealed a significant effect of Acoustic Similarity (F (1,21) = 81.26; $p < 0.001$). The interaction between Group and Time of Test was also significant (F (1,21) = 6.81; $p < 0.005$) supporting the view that there had been a selective benefit from rehearsal training. This interaction was explored further by an analysis of simple main effects. This revealed that there had been a significant increase in memory span in both the Rehearsal Trained Group (F (1,42) = 10.34; $p < 0.05$) and in the Repeatedly Tested Control Group (F (1,42) = 7.01; $p < 0.05$), but that there had been no significant increase in the Unseen Control Group (F (1,42) = 1.85; N.S.). This is an interesting result showing that simply testing subjects repeatedly on the memory span test resulted in improvements in performance.

There was also a significant interaction between Time of Test and Acoustic Similarity (F (1,21) = 12.48; $p < 0.002$), showing that the acoustic-similarity effect tended to be larger on the second than the first test. The most critical effect in this analysis, however, is the three-way interaction between Group, Time of Test, and Acoustic Similarity, which

TABLE 6.1

Average Spans (and Ranges) for Acoustically Similar (AS) and Acoustically Dissimilar (AD) Words for the Three Groups of Subjects at the Beginning and End of the Experiment

	Pre-Test		Post-Test	
	AS	AD	AS	AD
Trained Group	2.84	3.45	2.95	4.02
	(2.38–3.50)	(3.0–4.25)	(2.13–3.89)	(3.13–5.5)
Repeatedly Tested Control Group	2.63	3.34	2.59	3.47
	(2.13–3.13)	(2.5–4.0)	(2.13–3.5)	(2.63–4.63)
Unseen Control Group	2.73	3.17	2.60	3.1
	(2.4–3.4)	(2.6–3.45)	(2.5–3.0)	(2.6–4.1)

was also significant ($F(2,21) = 4.28$; $p < 0.02$). This interaction appears to be due to the tendency for the acoustic-similarity effect to increase in size more in the Rehearsal Trained Group than the two control groups. To explore this effect further a two-way analysis of variance on the difference scores between span for the similar and dissimilar lists was conducted. This revealed a significant interaction between Group and Time of Testing ($F(2,21) = 4.28$; $p < 0.02$). This interaction was explored by computing an analysis of simple main effects, which showed that the size of the acoustic-similarity effect increased in the Rehearsal Trained Group ($F(1,42) = 5.08$; $p < 0.05$), but not in either of the control groups (both Fs < 1.0).

Digit Span: The average digit spans for the three groups on each test are shown in Table 6.2. These scores give a measure of the extent to which any effects of training on the acoustically similar and dissimilar lists have generalized to other materials. It seems from these results that there is an increase in digit span in both the Rehearsal Trained and Repeatedly Tested Group; the increase being larger in the former group.

The digit span scores were entered into a two-way analysis of variance in which the factors were Group and Time of Test. This analysis revealed a significant effect of Time of Test ($F(1,21) = 6.84$; $p < 0.02$) and a marginally significant interaction between Group and Time of Testing ($F(2,21) = 3.40$; $p < 0.053$). This interaction clearly reflects the fact that the increases in digit span scores tend to be larger in the Rehearsal Trained Group, however, an analysis of simple main effects failed to show a reliable increase in digit span in any of the three groups. It seems, therefore, that although there is some tendency for the increase in memory span to generalize to materials on which no explicit training or repeated testing has been given, this effect is too small to be considered significant in the present study.

TABLE 6.2
Average Digit Span (and Ranges) for the 3 Groups of
Subjects at the Beginning and End of the Experiment

	Pre-Test	Post-Test
Trained Group	3.75	4.14
	(3.0–4.88)	(3.25–5.5)
Repeatedly tested Control Group	3.56	3.77
	(2.75–4.5)	(2.5–4.88)
Unseen Control Group	3.53	3.51
	(3.4–4.4)	(3.1–4.25)

DISCUSSION

The results of this experiment provide support for the theoretical position we set out to test. Our idea was that by training we should be able to increase the use of the articulatory loop in people with severe learning difficulties. This, we argued, should lead to an overall increase in memory span, coupled with an increase in the size of the acoustic similarity effect, which is thought to depend upon the rehearsal of information within the loop. Our results have confirmed these predictions. The rehearsal training did succeed in producing a selective increase in memory span coupled with an increase in the size of the acoustic similarity effect.

The finding that it is possible to increase short-term memory span in people with severe learning difficulties is encouraging, as there can be no doubt that our subjects' short-term memory deficits were very severe. One unexpected effect in the present experiment was that the Repeatedly Tested Group also showed reliable increases in memory span. These increases were, however, smaller than in the Rehearsal Trained Group, and repeated testing did not increase the size of the acoustic-similarity effect. However, both groups showed an increase in absolute levels of performance and a tendency for the acoustic-similarity effect to increase in size at the end of the experiment. The absence of a reliable increase in the size of the acoustic-similarity effect in the Repeatedly Tested Group most probably reflects a range effect, because the overall amount of improvement shown by this group was less than in the group trained to rehearse. In other words, we might expect that, given enough experience of being repeatedly tested on the memory span task, our subjects would show a significant increase in the size of the acoustic-similarity effect.

The fact that the repeated testing given to the control group appears to have improved their memory span and increased the efficiency of their utilization of the articulatory loop is an important result. The intensive practice on the memory span task seems to have led to improvements in the encoding and rehearsal of material in the articulatory loop. The overt rehearsal training was more effective even though it was very difficult for our subjects. It might be argued, however, that the simplicity of giving straightforward practice on the memory span task recommends it as a practical technique for improving short-term memory skills in people with severe learning difficulties.

The study reported here obviously raises a number of questions that could usefully be examined in future studies. One issue concerns the use of rehearsal training procedures as compared to mere rote training on memory span tasks. It remains unclear whether under different circumstances (if, for example, training occurred for longer with more able subjects) training in an overt cumulative rehearsal strategy would show greater superiority to mere rote practice on memory span tasks. To our surprise, it appears that the previous studies of rehearsal training, with subjects with moderate learning difficulties, have not employed control groups given equivalent practice on memory span tasks. It seems, therefore, that a general issue for studies in this area is to assess the relative merits of these two training procedures. It would seem that further studies over a longer time period comparing the effectiveness of rehearsal training with simple practice on memory span tasks would be worthwhile.

Another issue concerns possible variations in the effectiveness of training memory span at different ages. The teenagers who participated in our experiment were nearing maturity. On the one hand, having a higher mental age may aid performance on relatively complex tasks such as rehearsal training, but on the other hand, it is also possible that greater gains could be obtained with younger subjects. From a practical point of view, it would be useful to look at the possible long-term benefits of training short-term memory skills in children with severe learning difficulties. We know quite clearly from evidence presented earlier that these children experience a profound failure of development in these skills. As development proceeds their short-term memory skills fall further and further behind other indices of cognitive growth. It is at least possible that training, if started early and continued long enough, could help to overcome this failure of development. If such an improvement could be achieved, it might also have some more general beneficial effects on other cognitive skills known to be related to the operation of short-term memory, such as reasoning, arithmetic, language, and reading skills.

CHAPTER 7

Working Memory and Severe Learning Difficulties: A Synthesis

RELATIONSHIPS BETWEEN STUDIES OF NORMAL AND ABNORMAL DEVELOPMENT

In general terms, studies of cognitive impairments in children with learning difficulties have at least three possible purposes. First, they contribute to an understanding of the nature of learning difficulties. This is important theoretically, and in practical terms may lead to better ways of planning education: If we wish to design educational methods to ameliorate these children's difficulties, it is important to know as much as possible about the nature of their difficulties and the mechanisms responsible for them.

A second justification for studying cognitive impairments is that such studies may help us to understand the processes responsible for cognitive development. In our case we are particularly interested in the mechanisms responsible for short-term memory and its development. We will consider later the ways in which the studies reported here have contributed to an understanding of the mechanisms responsible for memory development.

A third reason for studying cognitive impairments (and the development of cognitive processes in general) is to contribute to our theoretical understanding of cognitive processes. Most obviously, if theories of cognitive processes, usually developed on the basis of studies of adults, are unable to handle data from developmental studies and studies of cognitive impairments (whether developmental or acquired) these theories are inadequate and will need to be revised to take account of such data (cf. Hulme, 1986).

We will consider the implications of the present work in relation to each of these broad themes.

AN OVERVIEW OF MAJOR FINDINGS

It is appropriate to take stock of our major findings before going on to consider their implications. We began by considering the nature of cognitive deficits found in children with learning difficulties. All of our work has focused on analyzing the short-term memory impairments experienced by children with severe learning difficulties (those with IQs below 50). Before the present work it was known that children with severe learning difficulties experience short-term memory problems. No previous studies, however, had looked at the pattern of development of short-term memory skills in these children. We have found that severe learning difficulties are characterized by a profound lack of development in short-term memory skills. This means that as these children get older, their short-term memory skills lag further and further behind many of their other cognitive skills. This is a striking pattern, given these children's generally slow rate of cognitive development across the board.

Subsequent experiments have shown that these difficulties seem explicable in terms of a failure, or inability, to utilize the articulatory loop, a speech-based rehearsal mechanism that is a major determinant of immediate memory span. On a more optimistic note, in the previous chapter it has been shown that these short-term memory problems, even when severe, can at least be reduced by training. Somewhat surprisingly, we found that giving rote practice in memory span tasks was almost as effective as a more elaborate rehearsal training strategy.

THE NATURE OF SEVERE LEARNING
DIFFICULTIES AND THE ROLE OF
WORKING MEMORY DEFICITS

It remains for us to consider the status of our findings concerning short-term memory deficits in people with severe learning difficulties. To put the question bluntly, have the short-term memory impairments got anything to do with the origins of these people's learning difficulties? Without the view of short-term memory as a working memory system, an immediate answer to this question would, no doubt, be: No, not much! However, the working memory view suggests that the short-term memory deficits found in people with severe learning difficulties could play a role in causing some of their learning difficulties. This is a possibility that we need to consider seriously, but perhaps also cautiously.

Children with severe learning difficulties, by definition, show massive impairments on almost all cognitive tasks. In the light of this, a sceptic might argue that their problems with verbal serial recall tasks of the sort studied here are amongst the least of their problems. For many years the most usual example of the importance of short-term memory was as a temporary holding system used when remembering a phone number for long enough to dial it. Such a view would not lead one to expect impairments on such a task to have important consequences! The development of the working memory framework, however, leads us to consider much more seriously the possibility that the capacity of short-term storage may place important limitations upon other cognitive skills. If serial recall tasks, such as digit span, tap a limited capacity system (or systems) that is also involved in the storage and manipulation of verbal material during more complex tasks, such as reading and comprehending prose, reasoning, and mental arithmetic, then it becomes very likely that impairments in such a system will have important consequences for the learning and performance of other more important skills. In the light of these ideas it is appropriate to consider evidence for the importance of short-term memory as a working memory system in the performance of more complex skills.

WORKING MEMORY AND READING COMPREHENSION

The largest body of evidence relevant to the role of short-term memory as a working memory system comes from studies of reading. Historically, there has been a close association between studies of short-term memory and reading. Most of the evidence comes from studies of adults; we will consider possible differences between adults and children later.

There are three main strategies that have been used to find support for the view that short-term memory functions as working memory system. The first is to look at the effects of interference. If the operation of working memory can be disrupted, then we should expect it to have detrimental effects on tasks where working memory is important. A second approach involves looking at individual differences. If working memory places limitations on the efficiency of other processes, then other things being equal, individuals with good working memory systems should be good at these other tasks. The research strategy here is basically to look for correlations between measures of working memory and reading skill.

A third, and in some ways related approach, comes from neuropsychology. Some patients, following brain injury, show severe deficits on short-term memory tasks. It can then be asked whether they show deficits in other skills, such as reading, where working memory storage is allegedly important. This approach is akin to the individual differences strategy, in so far as the patients studied could be seen as being very extreme cases of individuals with poor short-term memory skills. In other ways, perhaps, the approach is distinct, particulary in its emphasis on the virtues of single case studies rather than studies of groups. In what follows we will not try to review this large body of evidence exhaustively, but rather deal with some key studies and their implications for the present argument.

The first type of study was pioneered by Baddeley and Hitch (1974) in their earliest work on working memory. They applied techniques known to disrupt short-term memory storage, and observed the effects on other tasks including reading. A representative study of this sort is by Baddeley, Eldridge, and Lewis (1981). Here, subjects were required to read prose passages and detect errors of word order which had been introduced. Subjects either performed the task silently, whilst performing articulatory suppression or, as a control for the attentional demands of performing suppression, whilst tapping on the table. The results showed that suppression increased subjects' error rate on this task. This could be taken as evidence for the role of working memory in reading, but only if the task is accepted as representative of normal reading, and if we accept that tapping is an adequate control for the non-specific attentional demands of articulatory suppression. Detecting errors of word order clearly is not "normal reading" but, perhaps it is reasonable to accept that the processes involved in this task share considerable overlap with those normally involved in reading prose. The question of the specificity of the interference is much more difficult. How do we assess to what extent suppression produces general decrements in performance (doing two things is always more difficult than doing just one) rather than specific effects on verbal working memory?

This question was taken up by Waters, Caplan, and Hildebrandt (1987). They compared the effects of articulatory suppression with the effects of tapping on subjects' ability to decide whether sentences were semantically acceptable or not. The sentences used varied in their degree of complexity. In order to check whether the tapping and articulation tasks were of about the same overall level of difficulty, the decrement in performance produced by each task was compared on a third irrelevant task that did not seem to share any specific processes with reading, tapping or articulation. They found that articulatory suppression interfered with subjects' ability to make judgements about the sentences whereas the tapping task did not. This seems good support for the importance of the articulatory loop in the processes involved in reading and understanding sentences.

A similar conclusion comes from a recent experiment by Coltheart, Avons, and Trollope (1990). In this experiment, subjects read sentences and were asked to decide whether they were semantically acceptable or not. Some of the unacceptable sentences contained words that were homophonic with words that would have made the sentences acceptable. (So, for example, if the acceptable sentence was "The palace had a *throne* room" a possible corruption of the sentence might be "The palace had a *thrown* room"). It was found that the unacceptable sentences containing misleading homophones were more likely to be accepted as correct than control sentences containing an unacceptable word that was visually, but not phonologically similar, to the acceptable word, e.g. "The palace had a *thorns* room". People appear to be generating and using some sort of phonological code in the process of making their sentence acceptability judgements. Furthermore, when people performed articulatory suppression, the homophonic confusion effect was abolished. In a control experiment suppression was also shown to abolish the word-length effect in a serial recall task. Thus, the phonological code that is involved in making the sentence acceptability judgements is seen to be the same one as is responsible for the word-length effect in short-term memory. This is further evidence for the role of the articulatory loop in reading and comprehending sentences.

Working Memory and Individual Differences In Reading Ability

A working memory framework makes it natural to expect that variations in short-term memory skills will be related to variations in reading skill. Until recently, however, it has proved difficult to find support for this idea.

One influential study of this issue was conducted by Perfetti and Goldman (1976). They compared the performance of a group of good and poor readers on two memory tasks. One was a probed serial recall task using random digit lists, the other involved probed serial recall of words from sentences. It was found that the two groups differed on probed recall from the sentences but not from the digit lists. It was concluded that short-term memory differences were not important in accounting for differences in reading skill within the normal range. One problem in accepting this conclusion, however, is that the probed serial recall task was very difficult and the low levels of performance obtained may have served to minimize true differences between the two groups.

These results, and others like them, prompted Daneman and Carpenter (1980) to attempt to devise more adequate tests of working memory to see if more robust relationships with reading ability would emerge. They devised a measure called "reading span". In this task subjects had to read a series of sentences and memorize the final word in each. They began with sequences of two sentences and the number presented increased until subjects were no longer able to recall the terminal words in correct serial order. Daneman and Carpenter gave this task, and a conventional memory span task for unrelated words, to a group of 20 undergraduates. The reading span task correlated highly with two different measures of reading comprehension (r = 0.72 and 0.90) and a further study showed that equivalent results were obtained with another measure where subjects listened to the sentences instead of reading them. The conventional word span measure produced lower correlations (r = 0.37 and 0.33), which, because of the small sample size, were not significant. However it should be pointed out that correlations of 0.33 and 0.37 are hardly trivial especially when we consider that this study used a highly selected group of subjects (Carnegie-Mellon undergraduates). Restrictions in the range of abilities present in such a group will naturally tend to reduce the magnitude of any correlations obtained.

These studies do not give a clear picture of the relationship between short-term memory and reading ability. The Daneman and Carpenter study used a small group of subjects of high ability but nevertheless obtained correlations in excess of 0.30 between memory span for words and reading comprehension scores. It seems likely that because of sampling restrictions this may be an underestimate of the true size of the relationship. The absence of a clear relationship between short-term memory and differences in reading ability in the Perfetti and Goldman study, on the other hand, may reflect the use of an atypical and very difficult measure of memory.

With these considerations in mind we have recently conducted a developmental study of the relationship between short-term memory and reading skill (Hulme, 1988). One idea that lay behind this study was that the importance of short-term memory as a limiting factor for other cognitive skills may well change developmentally. We know that the effective capacity of short-term memory changes dramatically between early and middle childhood; because short-term memory capacity is limited at younger ages it may be more of an information processing bottleneck.

We saw 40 7- and 8-year-olds and 43 9- and 10-year-olds. Each child received a number of tests; reading comprehension was assessed using the Neale Analysis of Reading Ability (Neale, 1966), and language comprehension using the TROG test (Bishop, 1982); a short form of the WISC provided an estimate of IQ for each child. Short-term memory was assessed using short, medium, and long words following procedures developed in our earlier studies of memory development (Hulme et al., 1984).

The main results of interest from the present perspective are the correlations between memory span and reading ability. We had expected that the correlation between memory span and reading ability would be lower in the older group of children. A measure of span was obtained by averaging across the words of different lengths. The correlation between memory span and reading comprehension was $r = 0.57$ for the younger group and $r = 0.45$ in the older group. Although the correlation is slightly lower in older subjects as predicted, the difference between these correlations is not statistically significant. Nevertheless, the magnitude of both these correlations is substantial and further analyses showed that the correlation between span and reading comprehension remained significant even when the effects of age, IQ, and language comprehension ability were partialled out ($r = 0.305$ and 0.277; $p < 0.05$). Thus, even on this rather conservative analysis, short-term memory skills are shown to be related to differences in reading ability in this age range.

These results show that, even within the normal range of ability, short-term memory correlates with reading ability in children. There is also ample evidence that dyslexic children typically do poorly on digit span tests and other measures of short-term memory (these studies have been reviewed by Hulme, 1981, 1987; Jorm, 1983) although not all such children have poor short-term memories (Torgesen, Rashotte, Greenstein, Houck, & Portes, 1987). It has also been argued that the working memory deficits found in children with reading difficulties may cause difficulties with higher-level text comprehension processes in these children (see, for example, Macaruso, Bar-Shalom, Crain, & Shankweiler 1989; Shankweiler & Crain, 1986; Hulme & Snowling, in press, a).

In summary, there is clear evidence that in normal children individual differences in short-term memory capacity correlate with reading skill. Even in Daneman and Carpenter's group of high-ability subjects memory span for words correlated with reading skill. In our own studies with children we found higher correlations between memory span and reading ability. This suggests that short-term memory capacity may be more of a limiting factor on reading skill in children than in adults. Such a conclusion needs further data to support it, however. There are numerous differences between our own studies and those of Daneman and colleagues that could explain the differences in results obtained.

Nevertheless, for the present time it seems safe to conclude that memory span shows a reliable association with reading skill. This is consistent with a theory that suggests a causal link between short-term memory skills and reading skill. The evidence here, however, is purely correlational and so we cannot conclude a causal link between memory and reading exists.

WORKING MEMORY AND LEARNING

The correlational evidence, and the effects of articulatory suppression discussed above, address the question of whether working memory supports the performance of certain skills. A different question, of great importance, that so far has received less interest is whether working memory is important for learning new skills and new knowledge.

Perhaps the first evidence that working memory may play such a role came from neuropsychology. Baddeley, Papagno, and Vallar (1988) studied a patient, PV, who had a severe and pure deficit of verbal short-term memory. PV was able to learn to associate pairs of words in her native language (Italian) normally. This is evidence for normal associative learning between existing entries in verbal long-term memory. PV, however, was grossly impaired in learning to associate known words with novel words from a foreign language (Russian). The words chosen were two and three syllable Russian words, PV could repeat the two syllable words perfectly, but made around 20% errors on the three syllable words. With auditory presentation she was completely unable to learn to respond with the appropriate Russian word when prompted with its Italian associate, with visual presentation her performance improved but was still clearly impaired. These results suggest that severe impairments of short-term memory of the sort found in PV impair the long-term learning of phonological information. This perhaps is not surprising, but nor is it obvious that such an effect should occur. Baddeley et al. argue that some form of maintenance of information in working memory (or more specifically in the phonological input store of the revised working memory model) is necessary for learning the phonological form of new words. We will consider possible developmental implications of these results below.

A related line of research with children has been pursued by Gathercole and Baddeley (1989). They used a non-word repetition task as a measure of phonological storage. They conducted a longitudinal study with 104 children, starting when the children were aged between 4 and 5 years. As well as measuring non-word repetition, non-verbal intelligence was assessed using Raven's Progessive Coloured Matrices; receptive vocabulary skills were assessed using the short form of the

British Picture Vocabulary Test; and reading skills were assessed using the British Abilities Scales word reading test.

The scores on the non-word repetition test were found to correlate highly with vocabulary scores on the BPVS at the first test (age 4) and a year later (age 5). These relationships were maintained after partialling out the effects of non-verbal intelligence and age. The correlation between repetition performance at age 4 and vocabulary scores at age 5 was also shown to hold up even when, in addition to these other variables, vocabulary at age 4 was partialled out.

Gathercole and Baddeley (1989) argue that their non-word repetition task provides a measure of "phonological memory" and that this explains its ability to predict vocabulary development. This is by direct analogy with the argument made for PV's difficulties learning new words. There are some difficulties with this argument. Traditional measures of phonological short-term memory involve memory for sequences of familiar words as in digit span. In the case of repeating individual unknown non-words, the processes involved clearly differ. In particular, the repetition of non-words, as well as phonological memory, requires the non-lexical processes of phonological segmentation, and assembly of articulatory instructions. Precisely this argument was made by Snowling, Goulandris, Bowlby, and Howell (1986) following their study of non-word repetition deficits in dyslexic children. These same children are known to suffer from delays in the acquisition of naming skills. Snowling et al. argued that the non-word repetition difficulties reflected difficulties with phoneme segmentation and possibly assembly of articulatory instructions. This, they argued, could delay the acquisition of long-term phonological representations of words, as assessed in tasks such as picture naming (cf. Snowling, Van Wagtendonk & Stafford, 1988).

Further difficulties for a direct alignment between non-word repetition and phonological memory in Gathercole and Baddeley's study were advanced by Snowling and Chiat (1990). They point to inconsistencies between Gathercole and Baddeley's data and a straightforward memory explanation. Gathercole and Baddeley used one, two, three, and four syllable non-words in their repetition task. Predictions from a memory hypothesis must be that these different non-words will show systematic increases in repetition difficulty as length increases. This was not found, however; repetition of one syllable words was only as good as repetition of three syllable words. Equally, from their own data, Snowling and Chiat point out that some of Gathercole and Baddeley's four syllable non-words were very easy to repeat.

Snowling and Chiat argue that these patterns of repetition performance reflect the similarity between the non-words and words that children know. They draw particular attention to the fact that non-words containing morphemes (e.g. thick*ery*) give cues to their prosodic structure and hence pronunciation. Thus, children with good knowledge of the morphological, and phonological (including prosodic) structure of words will be at an advantage when presented with non-words to repeat. In this way, Snowling and Chiat turn the argument on its head: children with good vocabulary knowledge are better able to cope with the processing demands of non-word repetition tasks than are children with poor vocabulary knowledge.

These arguments were taken up by Gathercole, Willis, Emslie, and Baddeley (1991), who re-analyzed some of the data from their non-word repetition task. To examine the effects of linguistic structure on repetition they measured three attributes of the non-words: (1) the number of derivational morphemes in each item; (2) the number of root morphemes in each item; and (3) the word-likeness of each item as rated by adults on a scale from one to five. They found that when the effects of these three measures had been controlled for statistically, the effects of non-word length still had significant effects on repetition accuracy and conclude "that phonological memory ... places significant constraints on non-word repetition". This conclusion is unwarranted, however, because as Snowling, Chiat, and Hulme (1991) point out, the effects of length in such an analysis cannot simply be attributed to the effects of memory. Longer items, as well as being harder to remember, will also place greater demands upon other phonological processes, such as segmentation and the assembly of articulatory motor programs. Gathercole et al. also found that their word-likeness ratings did correlate significantly with repetition accuracy. This shows that linguistic structure is important to the process of non-word repetition.

In sum, the efficiency of the processes tapped by non-word repetition is likely to place constraints on a child's ability to learn new vocabulary items. It seems wrong, however, simply to wrap these processes up together in the blanket term of phonological memory. It is possible that limitations on children's storage capacity for phonological information is one source of difficulty in non-word repetition and partially responsible for its correlation with vocabulary scores. It seems very likely from the arguments presented by Snowling, Chiat, and Hulme, however, that other components of this complex task are more crucial. The nature and origin of the relationship between non-word repetition ability and vocabulary knowledge is an important area for future research.

In summary, there is suggestive evidence that temporary storage capacity in verbal working memory plays a role in the learning of new phonological information. PV, a patient with a drastic impairment of span (digit or word span of between two and three items), also shows a severe impairment in learning new phonological information. The natural developmental implication of this finding is that temporary storage of phonological information plays a role in learning the phonological form of new words. It is notable, however, that PV's span is lower than even that of an average 4- or 5-year-old child. So it may not be safe to conclude that the variations in phonological memory skills found in normal children place constraints on the learning of new vocabulary. A further difficulty is arguing from an association of deficits: Are all patients with short-term memory deficits subject to similar impairments of long-term phonological learning, or is it just coincidental that PV has suffered damage to two separate skills? The developmental implications of PV's long-term learning difficulties have been pursued by Gathercole and Baddeley (1989) in the longitudinal study discussed earlier. It is unfortunate, however, that they did not include conventional measures of short-term memory performance as well as non-word repetition in their study. It has been argued that their finding of a correlation between non-word repetition and vocabulary knowledge most likely reflects more complex processes than the storage of phonological information. Theoretically, the separation of phonological storage processes from other phonological processes (such as segmentation, blending, and articulatory assembly) may prove very difficult. Achieving such a separation effectively is almost certain to depend on a better specification of the mechanisms responsible for phonological processing, in tasks such as memory span and non-word repetition. This, in turn, will require an integration of ideas about short-term memory and speech perception and speech production. These are complex theoretical issues to which we will return below.

DISSOCIATIONS BETWEEN WORKING MEMORY DEFICITS AND GENERAL LEARNING DIFFICULTIES

A possible problem for the argument being developed here, for a link between working memory skills and other aspects of cognitive development, comes from cases of apparent dissociations between these different areas in development. The clearest and best documented cases of this sort are cases of developmental dyslexia.

The first, and best known case of this sort, is that of RE, an undergraduate studied by Campbell and Butterworth (1985). RE's problems first came to notice because of her spelling difficulties. She spelled inaccurately and dysphonetically, and had apparently experienced difficulties in learning to read. Her reading as an undergraduate remained largely visually based, and she was unable to decode unfamiliar words. In short, she appeared to be a phonological dyslexic. RE had a digit span of four: This is very low in relation to her age and overall ability. Nevertheless, RE's reading and language comprehension skills were good, and she managed to graduate with a good honours degree.

A similar case to RE, who has been studied longitudinally, is JM a dyslexic boy (Snowling & Hulme, 1989). Like RE, JM's spelling errors were dysphonetic and he had great difficulties in decoding novel words. Nevertheless, JM was very bright with a full-scale IQ over 120, and his reading comprehension was consistently in advance of his decoding skills.

To investigate the nature of his impairment of verbal short-term memory, at age 12 years, JM's memory span for words of short, medium, and long spoken duration was assessed, as was his speech rate for these words, following procedures used in previous studies of memory development (Hulme & Tordoff, 1989; Hulme et al., 1984). The results of this were quite striking. His span for the short, medium, and long words was 3.75, 3.5, and 3.25 respectively; his speech rate for these words, in words per second was 1.75, 1.44, and 1.33 (Snowling & Hulme, 1989). JM's memory span and speech rate for these words was, therefore, roughly comparable to that of normal 5-year-olds (Hulme & Tordoff, 1989; Hulme et al., 1984). We also assessed JM's memory span for acoustically similar and dissimilar words in just the same way as for words of different lengths. Here again, performance was severely depressed and in line with that of normal 5-year-olds in the Hulme and Tordoff study; his span for acoustically dissimilar words was 3.75, for similar words 3.25. In contrast to JM's severe verbal short-term memory impairments, his visual memory skills were excellent, as assessed by his ability to remember abstract shapes which are difficult to name.

For present purposes, the important point to note is that both RE and JM showed severe impairments of verbal short-term memory, in conjunction with excellent cognitive skills in most other areas. They have both had severe difficulties in learning to read and cope with spelling-to-sound rules (this is particularly clearly documented in JM), but their reading and language comprehension skills remained essentially intact. Do these cases show that short-term memory skills are unimportant for most other aspects of cognitive development?

Our answer would be less extreme, but these cases certainly place limits on the extent to which we can claim short-term memory skills are in any way central to other aspects of cognitive development. We know that in both these cases short-term memory skills never developed properly, and that both JM and RE had excellent general ability. This, then, brings us to the knotty problem of compensatory strategies. It seems possible, and indeed likely, that these subjects have learned in atypical ways in order to minimize the impact of their short-term memory difficulties. There is clear evidence for this in the case of their reading skills, where learning seems to have proceeded without the usual back-up of phonic reading strategies (see Hulme & Snowling, in press, b; Snowling & Hulme, 1989, for further evidence and discussion of this). We can only speculate at the moment as to how equivalent compensatory strategies could have been used in the mastery of other skills. It is reasonable to suppose that the extent to which compensatory strategies can be used will depend on general ability. Intelligent people like JM and RE may be more able to learn in the absence of adequate short-term memory skills than other people of lower ability. Presumably, in people with severe learning difficulties, such compensatory strategies are severely limited.

The existence of good general cognitive skills in people with severe short-term memory problems places clear limits on theories about the relationship between short-term memory skills and cognitive development. A theory that sees good short-term memory skills as an essential prerequisite for the mastery of other skills, such as language and reading comprehension, clearly is not tenable. There may be, of course, some minimal level of short-term memory skill that is essential for the mastery of these and other skills, but evidence from RE and JM suggests that this is going to be at a low level, as they only had spans of between three and four short words.

It seems reasonable to suppose that compensatory strategies are important in cases of subjects with good general cognitive skills such as JM and RE. In subjects with general learning difficulties the existence of short-term memory problems may serve to compound their other difficulties due to a lack of compensatory strategies. A possible theoretical position would be that verbal short-term memory serves as a useful supplementary back-up system when immediate processing resources are exceeded, but that a severely limited system is quite sufficient for the acquisition and performance of many skills that are central to intelligent behaviour.

This view, from a developmental perspective, is essentially analogous to the position that Shallice (1989) has advanced in relation to the association between language comprehension deficits and short-term memory problems in patients following brain damage. Many patients with severe short-term memory impairments (such as PV mentioned earlier) show surprisingly good language comprehension skills. A view that sees language comprehension as dependent on the use of short-term memory as a working memory system, might expect language comprehension problems to be more common and more severe in these patients. Most (perhaps all?) of these patients do, however, show deficits on long, syntactically complex sentences. It is argued, therefore, that normally language comprehension occurs rapidly and automatically "on line" but that on occasions reference to a verbatim record of what was said is necessary to disambiguate certain phrases; this is where short-term memory becomes important. The relationship between short-term memory impairments and other skills in development is inherently more complex than in the case of the loss of skills in adulthood. As we argued earlier, the existence of longstanding impairments from early childhood raises the possibility of compensatory strategies resulting in development proceeding along an atypical course. We have very good evidence for this in the case of JM learning to read.

WORKING MEMORY DEFICITS AND COGNITIVE DEVELOPMENT IN SEVERE LEARNING DIFFICULTIES

As we noted earlier, children with severe learning difficulties have problems in acquiring a wide range of skills, and these certainly include those skills traditionally considered to place heavy demands upon working memory, such as language comprehension, reasoning, reading, and arithmetic. Is it reasonable to argue that these difficulties are dependent, even partially, upon their short-term memory deficits? The evidence on this issue is far from clear, and it seems to us that extreme caution is needed here.

On one level it is clear that the short-term memory problems of those with severe learning difficulties are almost certainly a consequence of more general language difficulties, or, more specifically, perhaps, difficulties with speech. This is particularly clear in the case of Down's syndrome (see Chapter 1). In this sense, then, we can say that the memory problems are secondary to a more general difficulty. Whilst accepting this, it is nevertheless possible to consider that the short-term memory deficits in turn compromise the acquisition and performance of other skills. In such a view causal influences are bi-directional, speech and language problems cause memory problems, which in turn contribute to causing deficits in other higher-level skills, such as reading comprehension, arithmetic, and reasoning. Our hypothesis then, is for short-term memory problems playing possibly only a minor contributory role to some of the cognitive problems associated with severe learning difficulties.

This causal hypothesis, we must emphasize, lacks any convincing evidence to support it at present. Proving causal relationships in development is always very difficult. One difficulty is that many of the tasks that have been used to investigate the role of working memory in performing other skills, such as interference tasks, are simply too difficult to give to people with severe learning difficulties. Further progress here is likely to depend upon a better understanding of the role of working memory skills in normal children. With better understanding of normal development, studies in this area could then probably most effectively be applied to children with moderate, rather than severe, learning difficulties in the first instance.

THE EDUCATIONAL IMPLICATIONS OF WORKING MEMORY DEFICITS IN SEVERE LEARNING DIFFICULTIES

The belief, yet to be confirmed, that the working memory deficits seen in children with severe learning difficulties contribute to their difficulties in acquiring educationally important skills, certainly has educational implications. The most obvious implication is that if such deficits could be ameliorated by training, this ought to have beneficial effects on other skills. This, of course, was the aim of the study reported in Chapter 6. It is certainly the case that the improvements found in that study were small. However, it was not supposed to be an educationally realistic examination of the potential benefits of training short-term memory skills. It is quite conceivable, indeed likely, that if training started earlier and was more extensive it would have larger effects. This would be an important question for future studies to address. For the moment we would emphasize that we are not advocating the widespread training of short-term memory skills in children with severe learning difficulties. A great deal more research is needed to assess the effectiveness and potential benefits of such training.

The other implication of the working memory impairments characteristic of those with severe learning difficulties is for teaching methods and teacher training. It may be possible, given an awareness of these problems, to modify teaching methods so as to minimize the demands placed on working memory skills. The most obvious implications of this view are for the style of language used in teaching. Long, complex sentences may overload the working memory capacity of those with severe learning difficulties. The use of short, simple sentences, which omit redundant or unessential information, will place fewer demands on working memory. Asking pupils to repeat instructions immediately after hearing them serves as a check on comprehension and memory.

Research into the educational attainments of people with severe learning difficulties is rather limited, and the little research that there has been, has tended to focus on Down's syndrome. One area where working memory skills are likely to be important is in learning to read. Buckley (1985) reviews research studies concerned with the learning of reading in Down's syndrome subjects. A number of studies show that reading skills in those with Down's syndrome tend to be higher than expected given their low IQs. It appears that Down's subjects learn to read using a primarily visual approach, reading errors often include semantic errors (e.g. reading "boat" for "ship"), whereas they lack phonic decoding skills, (Buckley & Wood, 1983). Buckley argues that these children are unable to benefit from phonics instruction and that they are best taught by a "look and say" method which places heavy emphasis on word meaning. A deficiency in phonic skills would, of course, be expected in subjects with such severe short-term memory problems, because holding partially decoded words in memory and blending them places heavy demands on short-term memory. The evidence about reading skills in Down's syndrome is, therefore, entirely consistent with the hypothesis that their short-term memory deficits place constraints on their acquisition of reading skills, even at the single word level. On the other hand, the evidence suggests that these people may use their relative strength in visual memory to read by a "direct" visual route, circumventing the use of phonics.

It is also interesting to note that a number of teachers have advocated the use of reading as a way of improving language skills in people with Down's syndrome. Duffen (1976) reports observations made when teaching his Down's syndrome daughter, Sarah, to read. Apparently, learning sentences in reading enabled her to produce sentences in her speech that she had been unable to master by simple repetition. This is consistent with evidence we reviewed earlier for deficits in visual memory in Down's syndrome subjects being less marked than for auditory material. It may be that the use of a visual memory code for material that is read serves to help overcome their severe verbal memory deficits.

Arithmetic and number skills is the other obvious area where working memory impairments are likely to have consequences for education. We have less evidence here than in the case of reading (Buckley, 1985), but it appears that the learning of number skills is harder for those with severe learning difficulties than is learning to read (e.g. Thorley & Wood, 1979). Learning number skills, especially in the early stages, relies upon the storage and manipulation of verbal information in working memory (as, for example, in counting a set of objects, or learning to count by rote). The existence of severe short-term memory limitations in people with severe learning difficulties may well place limitations on the acquisition of these basic number skills. Teaching methods may need to be modified to take account of short-term memory limitations by, for example, using dual visual and auditory presentation or shared counting between pupil and teacher (where the pupil and teacher articulate the numbers simultaneously).

RELEVANCE OF BASIC RESEARCH TO EDUCATION

One final issue that deserves some discussion is the relationship between basic research into cognitive processes and their impairments, as represented by the studies reported here, and education. As will be apparent, our view is that the relationship is an indirect one. As psychologists studying severe learning difficulties our concern has been with understanding cognitive processes, and their impairments. When such impairments are identified, they undoubtedly have educational implications. Those implications do not take the form of direct prescriptions for action, however. The two implications drawn out above derive from different views about how to cope with any putative deficit.

Training amounts to an attempt to teach out the deficit. This head-on approach is almost certainly a good one if it works; but it is difficult and may fail. Modifying teaching, our second strategy, in a sense amounts to teaching round the deficit. Given a difficulty it may be possible to acknowledge its existence and then try to minimize its impact. In practice, we suspect, a judicious mixture of both approaches will often work best. This, however, is an educational issue. The psychological evidence in this case (or any others we know of) does not lead directly to prescriptions for teaching. Such evidence, nevertheless, is important in highlighting the options available. Psychological theories have also been central to the development of training procedures. It is necessary, however, to emphasize the difference in approach between psychological and educational studies. The studies reported here have raised a number of educational questions about how to optimize learning in children with severe learning difficulties. Much further research is needed to explore these educational questions and find answers to them.

MODELS OF THE STRUCTURE OF WORKING MEMORY AND ITS DEVELOPMENT

Articulatory Skills and Short-term Memory Development

One of the most important theoretical threads running through this work, is the link between the development of articulatory skills and the development of short-term memory. As the work reviewed in Chapter 2 makes clear, there is very strong evidence from studies of normal children for a close and quantitative link between changes in the speed of speaking and changes in the capacity of short-term memory. This slightly surprising finding makes sense within the theoretical framework of Baddeley and Hitch's (1974) working memory model, and more specifically provides important additional support for the idea of the articulatory loop. Because the articulatory loop is subject to passive loss of information over time, rehearsal is necessary to refresh the decaying traces of items held on the loop. Factors that affect the rate at which the reactivation of articulatory traces can occur will, therefore, affect storage in such a system. There are really two kinds of variables that have been used to examine this: variations in materials (words of different lengths); and variations amongst subjects (variations in speech rate both within and between age groups). We would argue that the ability of the articulatory loop to provide a coherent and unitary explanation of both types of variable makes it the most successful model of verbal short-term memory. The model certainly provides the best explanation, to date, of developmental improvements in short-term memory.

Relating these ideas to the explanation of short-term memory problems in children with severe learning difficulties has resulted in a new explanation for these difficulties. As the studies in Chapter 5 demonstrated, markers for the operation of the articulatory loop, the effects of word length and acoustic similarity, were absent or severely attenuated in our sample of subjects with severe learning difficulties.

These results, then, point to deficits in the operation of the articulatory loop. Our favoured interpretation has been in terms of a failure to employ rehearsal. This would lead to an abolition of the word-length effect and a decrement in the size of the acoustic-similarity effect. However, as was pointed out earlier, articulation is not only involved in the process of rehearsal in the articulatory loop. According to the working memory model, articulation is also necessary for the encoding of visually presented material onto the loop. Furthermore, we argued in

Chapter 5 that articulation may also be involved in the retrieval of information stored in the loop. To take the explanation of deficits in short-term memory found in people with severe learning difficulties further, we need to consider ideas about the operation of the articulatory loop in more detail, and go on to consider some possible limitations to the working memory model that has guided our experiments.

An interesting, and possibly informative, analogy can be drawn between the performance of people with severe learning difficulties and normal subjects' performance on short-term memory tasks under conditions of articulatory suppression. In such studies, the subject is required to intone some irrelevant words such as "the,the,the" whilst holding other words in short-term memory. Not surprisingly, articulatory suppression dramatically impairs short-term memory performance. More interestingly, however, it also has selective effects on recall of different types of material. With visual presentation both the word-length and acoustic similarity effect are abolished by suppression; with auditory presentation although the word-length effect is abolished the acoustic similarity effect remains, albeit in an attenuated form. This pattern with auditory presentation, therefore, is exactly analogous to our findings from subjects with severe learning difficulties. This close parallel, in turn, provides converging evidence for our favoured interpretation of these short-term memory problems reflecting a deficit in rehearsal, as suppression is traditionally interpreted as a means of disrupting rehearsal.

It is appropriate now to consider in some more detail differing views about the operation of the articulatory loop and how best to interpret the effects of word length, acoustic similarity, and their interaction with articulatory suppression (Baddeley, 1986; Hulme & Tordoff, 1989). An evaluation of this evidence is central to our interpretation of the short-term memory impairments in severe learning difficulties.

The Effects of Articulatory Suppression and Models of the Articulatory Loop

In the original formulation of the articulatory loop (Baddeley & Hitch, 1974) the effects of acoustic similarity and word length were attributed to the operation of the same unitary articulatory loop system. In this view these two factors affected the same system, in slightly different ways. Word length was seen as affecting the time taken to rehearse material within the loop. Because long words take longer to say and so to rehearse, fewer could be stored within the decay time of the loop. Acoustic similarity, in this view, could simply be explained as affecting the discriminability of traces within the articulatory loop. Because acoustically similar words necessarily led to the creation of similar traces in the loop they would be more difficult to discriminate from each other than traces of dissimilar items. At this time, subtle differences between the effects of articulatory suppression on the occurrence of the acoustic similarity effect and word length effect according to modality of presentation were not recognized. The abolition of both effects following visual presentation could easily be handled within such a view by appealing to the fact that articulation was necessary to encode information into an articulatory code. In the absence of articulation, visually presented materials simply could not be encoded onto the loop.

Recently, a more complicated view of the articulatory loop has been formulated by Baddeley (1986; Salame & Baddeley, 1982). In this latest version of the model the interpretation of the acoustic similarity effect has been altered. According to this view the articulatory loop is now divided into two components, a passive phonological input store and an articulatory rehearsal loop. Here, auditory speech input gains obligatory access to the phonological store, while visual information is input via articulatory encoding in the rehearsal loop. The occurrence of the acoustic similarity is attributed to the passive input store, whereas the word-length effect depends upon the rehearsal loop. This then gives a way of explaining the interaction between articulatory suppression and the acoustic-similarity effect according to whether material is presented visually or auditorily. The effect of similarity is abolished when presentation is visual simply because it is never encoded into the phonological input store. When presentation is auditory, on the other hand, encoding into the phonological input store occurs automatically and hence a confusability effect is observed.

The other major piece of evidence that has led to the postulation of the two-component view of the articulatory loop is the unattended speech effect (Salame & Baddeley, 1982); memory for visually presented words is impaired by the simultaneous presentation of spoken material, which the subject is told, quite explicitly, to ignore. This effect is specific to speech (noise has very little effect) and is greater when the unattended speech is phonologically similar to the material to be remembered. The unattended-speech effect is seen as resulting from interference between the unattended speech and items that are being held in the phonological input store.

Throughout this book we have preferred interpretations of our data in terms of the earlier, unitary concept of the articulatory loop. This is not simply a matter of our being Luddites! Rather, we are persuaded that some results, particularly from studies of children, are better handled by the unitary view. The difference between the unitary view and the latest version of the articulatory loop centres on the necessity of postulating a phonological input store. How then can a unitary view handle the evidence concerning the existence of the unattended speech effect? Such an effect can in fact be interpreted quite simply by assuming that auditory speech input gains obligatory access to the articulatory loop. The simultaneous input of items in the unattended speech experiments simply leads to problems in encoding the visually presented material onto the loop (cf. Broadbent, 1984). The further observation that the effects of unattended speech are abolished by articulatory suppression can be explained in terms of suppression blocking access of visually presented material to the loop. This also explains why, with visual presentation, articulatory suppression abolishes the effects of word length (Baddeley et al., 1975), and acoustic similarity (see, e.g. Crowder, 1978).

This account admittedly leaves unspecified how it is that speech inputs manage to gain obligatory access to an articulatory representation. Clearly, there are many complex processes concerned with speech perception, and translation from abstract phonological to articulatory representations, that are left unspecified in such a schematic view. However, in this sense it is no more, or less, incomplete than the revised two-component view of the articulatory loop contained in the working memory model. To say that speech gains access to articulatory representations only via an input store is no more specific, than to say that speech perception processes (however they occur) have direct links to articulatory representations of the sort that can be rehearsed in an articulatory loop.

WHAT IS THE ARTICULATORY LOOP AND WHERE IS IT?

So far, the discussion of verbal coding in short-term memory has been conducted purely within the context of the working memory model and the concept of the articulatory loop. However, theories of short-term memory clearly need to make contact with theories of the processes responsible for speech perception and production. Self-evidently, our ability to listen to and then repeat a list of words requires the use of speech perception and production processes. The working memory model, in its present form, on the other hand, does not make any real contact with theories of these processes. Rather, it seems that the articulatory loop hangs, tenuously attached by two lines, to the central executive in something of a void! We need to consider how the concept of a rehearsal loop can be related to theories of speech perception and production.

An obvious starting point for such a discussion is with the logogen model of Morton (1969, 1970; Morton & Smith, 1974). The logogen model was developed as a way of conceptualizing a number of language skills, and particularly reading. The heart of the model, the logogen system, consisted of a set of logogen units, which essentially are coding units for all the words (or morphemes) that a subject knows. In the original model, common logogen units subserved both perception and production. In more recent versions of the model, separate logogen systems have been postulated for recognition and production and also for different input and output modalities (see, e.g. Morton, 1979). It is not necessary to deal with these complexities for the purposes of the present discussion.

A key component of the logogen model for explaining short-term memory phenomena is the response buffer. This system receives inputs from the logogen system and can also send outputs back to the logogen system. The response buffer is thought to hold information in the form of an articulatory code, and outputs from this system drive the process of articulation. The normal function of the response buffer is to allow the efficient programming of speech production. When outputs from the system are fed back to the logogen system this amounts to the process of silent rehearsal. This is, of course, the same process as embodied in the concept of the articulatory loop.

Evidence implicating the response buffer in errors in both spontaneous speech and short-term memory is reviewed by A. Ellis (1979). In spontaneous speech evidence for the role of a response buffer comes from speech errors, particularly Spoonerisms, where phonological segments of words are transposed or otherwise misordered, as in saying "Our *qu*eer old *D*ean" instead of "Our *d*ear old *Q*ueen". Such errors are evidence for the existence of pre-planned speech sequences being held is some form of phonological or pre-articulatory code. Studies of speech errors indicate that they are highly systematic in terms of the properties of the segments that are most often transposed, and similar factors have been shown to affect the misordering of items in short-term memory tasks. Thus, consonant segments are more often transposed than vowels, which are more often transposed than syllables, and syllable initial consonants tend to exchange with other syllable initial consonants rather than with syllable-final consonants, and vice versa. This pattern is observed in both speech errors and short-term memory errors (A. Ellis, 1979, 1980).

In summary, it is clear that the idea of an articulatory loop, as embodied in the working memory model, can be related to more general-purpose models of language use. The particular example that has been chosen to illustrate this is Morton's logogen model. It seems certain that a better understanding of short-term memory phenomena and their functional importance will result from attempts to unite their study with the study of other aspects of language use.

THE PROBLEMS WITH VERBAL THEORIES OF VERBAL SHORT-TERM MEMORY

There can be no doubt that verbally formulated theories, such as the working memory model and Morton's logogen model, have been useful in guiding experimental work. The experiments we have reported in earlier chapters we hope are evidence of how some relatively simple ideas from the working memory model have led to useful advances in understanding the short-term memory deficits found in severe learning difficulties. In more general terms, there can be no doubt that the model has led to important advances in our understanding of short-term memory phenomena, and has also helped to furnish an explanation of short-term memory development. We argued earlier that the explanation of short-term memory development in terms of changes in articulation speed within an articulatory loop, was certainly the most successful explanation for the growth of memory span to date.

Both the logogen model and working memory model are, however, subject to a criticism that has come to the fore recently: Both theories, it could be argued, suffer from a certain lack of explicitness. Verbally formulated theories of this sort are limited in the extent to which the processes they deal with are ever described explicitly. It is always possible to gloss over difficulties in these formulations by failing to specify how such difficulties might be overcome.

In contrast, a major attraction of computer simulation models is that glossing over complexities becomes more difficult. In such models, attempts are being made to write computer programs that simulate certain limited aspects of human performance. If they are to be implemented, such models have to make explicit decisions about many aspects of how the hypothetical system works. Recently, a number of theorists have set out to construct computationally explicit theories of short-term memory. It is not possible here to go into detail about the various approaches that have been adopted in these models (but see Brown & Hulme, in press, for an overview of these models). One model however, does come close to the approach outlined above in drawing on ideas concerning speech perception and speech production. This is the model developed by Brown (1990). In this model, the process of rehearsal is implemented by interfacing a mechanism for speech perception with one for speech production, (like the logogen model). Cycling information through these two interfaced systems amounts to a simplified model of sub-vocal rehearsal. Although incomplete in important respects, the model has been able to produce simulations of the effects of word length and acoustic similarity and the developmental relationship between speech rate and memory span.

Ultimately, we may hope that computational modelling will lead to more explicit and powerful models of speech perception, speech production, and memory processes. Such models will in turn provide a more precise language for describing the operation of short-term memory processes, the source of developmental improvements in these processes, and the nature of the impairments in these processes that have been documented in this book.

References

Anwar, F. (1981a). Motor function in Down's syndrome. *International Review of Research in Mental Retardation, 10,* 107-137.

Anwar, F. (1981b). Visual-motor target localisation in normal and subnormal development. *British Journal of Psychology, 72,* 43-57.

Atkinson, R.C. & Shiffrin, R.M. (1968). Human Memory: A proposed system and its control processes. In K.W. Spence (Ed.). *The psychology of learning and motivation: Advances in research and theory. Vol. 2.* New York: Academic Press.

Bachelder, B.L. & Denny, R. (1977). A theory of intelligence: I. Span and the complexity of stimulus control. *Intelligence, 1,* 127-150.

Baddeley, A.D. (1966). Short-term memory for word sequences as a function of acoustic, semantic and formal similarity. *Quarterly Journal of Experimental Psychology, 18,* 362-365.

Baddeley, A.D. (1983). Working memory. *Philosophical Transactions of the Royal Society of London, B, 302,* 311-324.

Baddeley, A.D. (1986). *Working memory.* London: Oxford University Press (Clarendon).

Baddeley, A.D., (1990). *Human memory: Theory and practice.* Hove: Lawrence Erlbaum Associates Ltd.

Baddeley, A.D., Eldridge, M., & Lewis, V.J. (1981). The role of subvocalisation in reading. *Quarterly Journal of Experimental Psychology, 33,* 439-454.

Baddeley, A.D. & Hitch, G. (1974). Working memory. In G.H. Bower (Ed.). *The Psychology of learning and motivation Vol. 8,* pp. 47-90. New York: Academic Press.

Baddeley, A.D. Lewis, V.J., & Vallar, G. (1984). Exploring the articulatory loop. *Quarterly Journal of Experimental Psychology, 36A,* 233-252.

Baddeley A.D., Papagno, C., & Vallar G. (1988). When long-term learning depends on short-term storage. *Journal of Memory and Language, 27,* 586-595.

Baddeley, A., Thomson, N., & Buchanan, M. (1975). Word length and the structure of short term memory. *Journal of Verbal Learning and Verbal Behaviour, 14*, 575-589.

Baumeister, A.A. & Bartlett, F.C. (1962). A comparison of the factor structure of normals and retardates on the WISC. *American Journal of Mental Deficiency, 67*, 257-261.

Belmont, J.M. (1966). Long-term memory in mental retardation. *International Review of Research on Mental Retardation, 1*, 219-255.

Belmont, J.M. (1972). Relations of age and intelligence to short term color memory. *Child Development, 43*, 19-29.

Belmont, I., Birch, H.G., & Belmont, L. (1967). The organisation of intelligence test performance in educable mentally subnormal children. *American Journal of Mental Deficiency, 71*, 969-976.

Belmont, J.M. & Butterfield, C.E. (1969). The relation of short term memory to development and intelligence. In L. Lipsett & H. Reese (Eds). *Advances in child development and behaviour. Vol. 4.* New York: Academic Press.

Belmont, J.M. & Butterfield, C.E. (1971). Learning strategies as determinants of mental deficiencies. *Cognitive Psychology, 2*, 411-420.

Benda, C.E. (1969). *Down's syndrome: Mongolism and its management.* New York: Grune & Stratten.

Berg, J.M. (1974). Aetiological aspects of mental subnormality: pathological factors. In A.M. Clarke & A.D.B. Clarke (Eds). *Mental deficiency: The changing outlook (3rd edn).* London: Methuen

Berkson, G. (1960). An analysis of reaction time in normal and mentally deficient young men. Parts I–III. *Journal of Mental Deficiency Research, 4*, 51-77.

Bilovsky, D. & Share, J. (1965). The Illinois Test of Pyscholinguistic ability and Down's Syndrome: An exploratory study. *American Journal of Mental Deficiency, 70*, 78-82.

Binet, A. & Simon, T. (1916). *The development of intelligence in children.* Baltimore: Williams & Wilkins.

Bishop, D.V.M. (1982). *TROG Test for Reception of Grammar.* Available from the author at the Department of Psychology, University of Manchester.

Boersma, F.J. & Muir, W. (1975). *Eye movements and information processing in mentally retarded children.* Rotterdam: Rotterdam University Press.

Borkowski J.G. & Cavanagh, J.C. (1979). Maintenance and generalisation of skills and strategies by the retarded. In N.R. Ellis (Ed.). *Handbook of mental deficiency* (2nd edn). Hillsdale, N.J.: Lawrence Erlbaum Associates Inc.

Brimer, M.A. & Dunn, L.M. (1973). *Administrative Manual, Full Range English Picture Vocabulary Test.* Bristol: Educational Evaluation Enterprises.

Broadbent, D.E. (1958). *Perception and communication.* London: Pergamon.

Broadbent, D. (1984). The Maltese Cross: a new simplistic model of human memory. *Behavioural and Brain Sciences, 7*, 55-94.

Brousseau, K., (1928). *Mongolism: a study of the physical and mental characteristics of mongolian imbeciles.* (Revised by Brainerd, H.G.) London: Baulliere, Tindall & Cox.

Brown, A.L., Campione, J.C., Bray, N.W., & Wilcox, B.L. (1973). Keeping track of changing variables: Effects of rehearsal training and rehearsal prevention in normal and retarded adolescents. *Journal of Experimental Psychology, 101*, 123-131.

Brown, A.L., Campione, J.C., & Murphy, M.D. (1974). Keeping track of changing variables: long term retention of a trained rehearsal strategy by retarded adolescents. *American Journal of Mental Deficiency, 78,* 446-453.

Brown, G.D.A. (1990). Short-term memory capacity limitations on recurrent speech production and perception networks. In *Proceedings of the eleventh annual conference of the cognitive science society.* Hillsdale, N.J.: Lawrence Erlbaum Associates Inc.

Brown G.D.A. & Hulme, C. (in press). Connectionist models of human short-term memory. In Omid. M. Omidvar (Ed.). *Progress in neural networks.* New Jersey: Ablex.

Brown, J. (1958). Some tests of the decay theory of immediate memory. *Quarterly Journal of Experimental Psychology, 10,* 12-21.

Buckley, S. (1985). Attaining basic educational skills: reading, writing and number. In D. Lane & B. Stratford (Eds.). *Current approaches to Down's syndrome.* London: Holt, Rhinehart & Winston.

Buckley, S. & Wood, E. (1983). *The extent and significance of reading skills in pre-school children with Down's syndrome.* Paper presented to the British Psychological Society, London.

Campbell, R. & Butterworth, B. (1985). Phonological dyslexia and dysgraphia in a highly literate subject; a developmental case with associated deficits of phonemic awareness and processing. *Quarterly Journal of Experimental Psychology, 37A,* 435-475.

Campione, J. & Brown, A.L. (1977). Memory and metamemory in educable retarded children. In R.V. Kail and J.W. Hagen (Eds.). *Perspectives on the development of memory and cognition.* Hillsdale, N.J.: Lawrence Erlbaum Associates.

Carr, J. (1975). *Young children with Down's syndrome.* London: Butterworths.

Carr, J. (1980). *Helping your handicapped child.* London: Penguin.

Carr, J. (1985). The development of intelligence. In D. Lane & B. Stratford (Eds). Current approaches to Down's syndrome. London: Holt, Rhinehart & Winston.

Case, R.D., Kurland, M., & Goldberg, J. (1982). Operational efficiency and the growth of short term memory span. *Journal of Experimental Child Psychology, 33,* 386-404.

Clarke, Ann M. & Clarke, A.D.B. (Eds.). (1974). *Readings from mental deficiency: The changing outlook. (3rd edn).* London: Methuen.

Clarke, A.D.B. & Clarke, Ann M. (1975). *Recent advances in the study of subnormality. (2nd edn).* London: MIND.

Coltheart, V., Avons, S.E., & Trollope, J. (1990). Articulatory suppression and phonological codes in reading for meaning. *Quarterly Journal of Experimental Psychology, 42A,* 375-399.

Conrad, R. (1964). Acoustic confusions in immediate memory. *British Journal of Pyschology, 55,* 75-84

Conrad, R. (1967). Interference or decay over short retention intervals? *Journal of Verbal Learning and Verbal Behavior, 6,* 49-54.

Conrad, R. (1971). Chronology of the development of covert speech in children. *Developmental Psychology, 5,* 398-405.

Conrad, R. & Hull, A.J. (1964). Information, acoustic confusion and memory span. *British Journal of Psychology, 55,* 429-432.

Cowan, N., Cartwright, C., Winterowd C., & Sherk M. (1987). An adult model of pre-school children's speech memory. *Memory & Cognition, 15*, 511-517.

Craik, F.I.M. (1970). Primary memory. *British Medical Bulletin, 27*, 232-236.

Cranefield, P. & Federn, W. (1967). The begetting of fools: an annotated translation of Paracelsus "De Generatione Stultorum". *Bulletin of the History of Medicine, 41*, 56-74, 161-174.

Crome, L., Cowie, V., & Slater, E. (1966). A statistical note on cerebellar and brain stem weight in mongolism. Journal of Mental Deficiency Research, 10, 69-72.

Crowder, R.G. (1978). Audition and speech coding in short-term memory: a tutorial review. In J. Requin (Ed.). *Attention and performance. Vol. 7*. Hillsdale, N.J.: Lawrence Erlbaum Associates Inc.

Cunningham, C. (1982). Psychological and educational aspects of handicap. In F. Cockburn & R. Gitzelman (Eds). *Inborn errors of metabolism*. Lancaster: MTP Press.

Daneman, M. & Carpenter, P.A. (1980). Individual differences in working memory and reading. *Journal of Verbal Learning and Verbal Behaviour, 19*, 450-466.

Das J.P. (1985). Aspects of digit span performance: Naming time and order memory. *American Journal of Mental Deficiency, 89*, 627-634.

Dodd, B. (1972). A comparison of babbling patterns in normal and Down's syndrome infants. *Journal of Mental Deficiency Research, 16*, 35-40.

Dodd, B. (1975). Recognition and reproduction of words by Down's syndrome and non-Down's syndrome retarded children. *American Journal of Mental Deficiency, 80*, 306-311.

Dodd, B. (1976). A comparison of the phonological systems of mental age matched normal, severely subnormal and Down's syndrome children. *British Journal of Disorders of Communication, 11*, 27-42.

Down, H., & Langdon, J. (1867). Observations on the ethnic classifications of idiots. *Journal of Mental Science, 13*, 121-123.

Drillien, C.M. (1963). Obstetric hazard, mental retardation and behaviour disturbance in primary school. *Developmental Medicine and Child Neurology, 5*, 3-13.

Duffen L. (1976). Teaching reading to children with little or no language. *Remedial Education, 11*, 139.

Ebbinghaus, H. (1885). *Memory: A contribution to experimental psychology.* (Translated by H.A. Ruger & C.E. Bussenius) New York: Columbia University.

Edwards, P. (1978). *Reading problems: Identification and treatment.* London: Heinemann.

Elliot, C. (1978). Factors influencing the response latencies of subnormal children in naming pictures. *British Journal of Psychology, 69*, 295-303.

Ellis, A. (1979). Speech production and short-term memory. In J. Morton & J. Marshall (Eds). *Psycholinguistics series. Vol. 2. Structures and processes.* Cambridge Mass.: MIT Press.

Ellis, A. (1980). Errors in speech production and short-term memory: The effects of phonemic similarity and syllable position. *Journal of Verbal Learning and Verbal Behavior, 19*, 624-634.

Ellis, N.C. & Hennelly, R.A. (1980). A bilingual word-length effect: Implications for intelligence testing and the relative ease of mental calculation in English and Welsh. *British Journal of Psychology, 71*, 43-51.

Ellis, N.R. (Ed.) (1963). The stimulus trace and behavioural inadequacy. In *Handbook of mental deficiency.* New York: McGraw-Hill.

Ellis, N.R. (1978). Do the mentally retarded have memory deficits? *Intelligence, 2,* 41-45.

Ellis, N.R. (1979) (Ed.). *Handbook of mental deficiency.* Hillsdale, N.J.: Lawrence Erlbaum Associates Inc.

Engle, R.W. & Marshall, K. (1983). Do developmental changes in digit span result from acquisition strategies? *Journal of Experimental Child Psychology, 36,* 429-436.

Fischler K. (1975). Mental development in mosaic Downs syndrome as compared with trisomy-21. In R. Koch & F. de la Cruz (Eds). *Downs syndrome (mongolism): Research, prevention and management.* New York. Bruner/Mazel.

Flavell, J.H. (1970). Developmental studies of mediated memory. *Advances in Child Development and Behaviour, 5,* 181-211.

Flavell, J.H. (1977). *Cognitive development.* New Jersey: Prentice Hall.

Flavell, J.H., Beach, D.R., & Chinsky, J.M. (1966). Spontaneous verbal rehearsal in a memory task as a function of age. *Child Development, 37,* 283-299.

Frith, U. & Frith, C.D. (1974). Specific motor disabilities in Down's syndrome. *Journal of Child Psychology and Psychiatry, 15,* 293-301.

Gath, A. (1981). Aging and mental handicap. *Developmental Medicine and Child Neurology, 28,* 519-22.

Gathercole, S., & Baddeley, A. (1989). Development of vocabulary in children and short-term phonological memory. *Journal of Memory and Language, 28,* 200-213.

Gathercole, S., Willis, C., Emslie, H., & Baddeley, A. D. (1991). The influences of number of syllables and wordlikeness on children's repetition of nonwords. *Applied Psycholinguistics, 12,* 357-368.

Gibson, D. (1978). *Down's syndrome: The psychology of mongolism.* Cambridge University Press.

Goddard, H.H. (1916). *Feeblemindedness; its causes and consequences.* New York: Macmillan.

Gregg, V.H., Freedman, C.M., & Smith, D.K. (1989). Word frequency, articulatory suppression and memory span. *British Journal of Psychology, 80,* 363-374.

Hanley J. R. & Broadbent, C. (1987). The effect of unattended speech on serial recall following auditory presentation. *British Journal of Psychology, 78,* 287-297.

Hebb, D.O. (1961). Distinctive features of learning in the higher animals. In J.F. Delafresnaye (Ed.). *Brain mechanisms and learning.* London: Oxford University Press.

Henderson, S. (1985). Motor skill development. In D. Lane & B. Stratford (Eds). *Current approaches to Down's syndrome.* London: Holt, Rhinehart & Winston.

Hitch, G.C. (1978). The role of short-term working memory in mental arithmetic. *Cognitive Psychology, 10,* 302-323.

Hitch, G.C. & Halliday, M.S. (1983). Working memory in children. *Philosophical Transactions of the Royal Society of London, B, 302,* 325-340.

Hitch, G.C., Halliday, M.S., & Littler J. (1989). Item identification speed and rehearsal rate as predictors of memory span in children. *Quarterly Journal of Experimental Psychology, 41A,* 321-37.

Hulme, C. (1981). *Reading retardation and multi-sensory teaching.* London: Routledge & Kegan Paul.

Hulme, C. (1984). Developmental differences in the effects of acoustic similarity on memory span. *Developmental Psychology, 20,* 650-652.

Hulme, C. (1986). Memory development: Interactions between theories in cognitive and developmental psychology. (Text of the 1985 Spearman Medal Lecture to the British Psychological Society.) *Bulletin of the British Psychological Society, 39,* 247-250.

Hulme, C. (1987). Reading retardation, In J.R. Beech & A.M. Colley (Eds.). *Cognitive approaches to reading.* Chichester: Wiley.

Hulme, C. (1988). Short-term memory development and learning to read. In M. Gruneberg, P. Morris, & R. Sykes (Eds). *Practical aspects of memory: Current research and issues.* Vol. 2. Clinical and educational implications. Wiley: Chichester.

Hulme, C. Maughan, S., & Brown, G.D.A. (1991). Memory for familiar and unfamiliar words: Evidence for a long-term memory contribution to short-term memory span. *Journal of Memory and Language, 30,* 685-701.

Hulme, C. & Muir, C. (1985). Developmental changes in speech rate and memory span: A causal relationship? *British Journal of Developmental Psychology, 3,* 175-181.

Hulme, C. & Snowling, M. (in press, a). Phonological deficits in dyslexia: A "sound" reappraisal of the verbal deficit hypothesis? In N. Singh & I. Beale (Eds.), *Progress in Learning Disabilities.* New York: Springer-Verlag.

Hulme, C. & Snowling, M. (in press, b). Deficits in output phonology: a cause of reading failure? *Cognitive Neuropsychology.*

Hulme, C., Thomson, N., Muir, C., & Lawrence, A. (1984). Speech rate and the development of short-term memory. *Journal of Experimental Child Psychology, 38,* 241-253.

Hulme, C. & Tordoff, V. (1989). Working memory development: The effects of speech rate, word length and acoustic similarity on serial recall. *Journal of Experimental Child Psychology, 48,* 1-19

Hulme, C., Silvester, J., Smith, S., & Muir, C. (1986). The effects of word length on memory for pictures: Evidence for speech coding in young children. *Journal of Experimental Child Psychology, 41,* 61-75.

Huttenlocher, J. & Burke, D. (1976). Why does memory span increase with age? *Cognitive Psychology, 8,* 1-31.

Jacobs, J. (1887). Experiments on prehension. *Mind, 12,* 75-79.

Jensen, A.R. (1981). Reaction time and intelligence. In M.P. Freidman, J.P. Das, & N. O'Connor (Eds.). *Intelligence and learning.* New York: Plenum.

Jorm, A.F. (1983). Specific reading retardation and working memory: A review. *British Journal of Psychology, 74,* 311-342.

Kail, R.V. (1984). *The development of memory in children. (2nd edn).* New York: W.H. Freeman.

Kail, R.V. (1990). *The development of memory in children. (3rd edn).* New York: W.H. Freeman.

Keeney, T.J., Cannizzo, S.R., & Flavell, J.H. (1967). Spontaneous and induced verbal rehearsal in a recall task. *Child Development, 38,* 953-966.

Klatzky, R. (1975). *Human memory.* New York: W.H. Freeman.

LaVeck, B. & Brehm, S.S. (1978). Individual variability among children with Down's syndrome. *Mental Retardation, 16,* 135-137.

Lejeune, J., Gautier, M., & Turpin, R. (1959). Les chromosomes humains en culture de tissus. *Comptes Rendues de l'Académie des Sciences, 248,* 602-603.

Lenneberg, E.H. (1967). *Biological foundations of language.* New York: Wiley.

Ludlow J.R. & Allen L.M. (1979). The effect of early intervention and pre-school stimulus on the development of the Down's syndrome child. *Journal of Mental Deficiency Research, 23,* 29-44.

Lyon, D.R. (1977). Individual differences in immediate serial recall: a matter of mnemonics? *Cognitive Psychology, 9,* 403-411.

Macaruso, P., Bar-Shalom, E., Crain, S., & Shankweiler, D. (1989). Comprehension of temporal terms by good and poor readers. Language and Speech, 32, 45-67.

Marcell, M.M., & Armstrong, V. (1982). Auditory and visual sequential memory of Down syndrome and nonretarded children. *American Journal of Mental Deficiency, 87,* 86-95.

Marinosson, G.L. (1974). Performance profiles of normal, E.S.N., S.S.N (matched M.A.) on the revised I.T.P.A. *Journal of Child Psychology and Psychiatry, 15,* 139-148

McDade, H.L. & Adler, S. (1980). Down's syndrome and short-term memory: a storage or retrieval deficit. American Journal of Mental Deficiency, 84, 561-567.

Miller, G.A. (1956). The magical number 7, plus or minus 2: some limits on our capacity for processing information. *Psychological Review, 63,* 81-97.

Milunsky, A. (Ed.). (1979). *Genetic disorders and the fetus: diagnosis, prevention and treatment.* New York: Plenum.

Mittler, P.J. (1974). Language and communication. In Ann M. Clarke & A.D.B. Clarke (Eds.). *Readings from mental deficiency: The changing outlook.* London: Methuen.

Morton J. (1969). The interaction of information in word recognition. *Psychological Review, 76,* 165-78.

Morton J. (1970). A functional model for human memory. In D.A. Norman (Ed.). *Models of human memory.* New York: Academic Press.

Morton, J. (1979). Facilitation in word recognition: Experiments causing change in the logogen model. In P. Kolers, M. Wrolstead, & H. Bouma (Eds.). *Processing of visible language. Vol. I.* New York: Plenum.

Morton, J. & Smith, N.V. (1974). Some ideas concerning the acquistion of phonology. In *Proceedings of the symposium on current problems in psycholinguistics.* Paris: CNRS.

Nakamura, H. (1961). Nature of institutionalised adult mongoloid intelligence. *American Journal of Mental Deficiency, 66,* 456-458.

Naveh-Benjamin, M. & Ayres, T.J. (1986). Digit span, reading rate, and linguistic relativity. *Quarterly Journal of Experimental Psychology, 38A,* 739-751.

Neale, M. (1966). *The Neale Analysis of Reading Ability.* London: MacMillan Education

Nicolson, R. (1981). The relationship between memory span and processing time. In M.P. Freidman, J.P. Das, & N. O'Connor (Eds.). *Intelligence and learning.* New York: Plenum.

Norman, D.A. (1970). *Models of human memory.* New York: Academic Press.

O'Connor, N. & Hermelin, B. (1973). The spatial or temporal organisation of short-term memory. *Quarterly Journal of Experimental Psychology, 25,* 335-343.

O'Connor, N. & Hermelin, B. (1978). *Seeing and hearing and space and time.* London: Academic Press.

Paraskevopoulos, J.N. & Kirk, S.A. (1969). *The development and pyschometric characteristics of the revised Illinois Test of Psycholinguistic Abilities.* Urbana: University of Illinois Press.

Perfetti, C.D. & Goldman, S.R. (1976). Discourse memory and reading comprehension skill. *Journal of Verbal Learning and Verbal Behaviour, 14,* 33-42.

Peterson, L.R. & Peterson, M.J. (1959). Short-term retention of individual items. *Journal of Experimental Psychology, 58,* 193-198.

Raine, A., Hulme, C., Chadderton, H., & Bailey, P. (1991). Verbal short-term memory span in speech disordered children: Implications for articulatory coding in short-term memory. *Child Development, 62,* 415-423.

Rectory Paddock School (1981). *In search of a curriculum: Notes on the education of mentally handicapped children.* Kent: Robin Wren Publications.

Rempel, E.D. (1974). Psycholinguistic abilities of Down's syndrome children. In *Proceedings of the Annual Meeting of the American Association on Mental Deficiency.* Toronto.

Richards, B.W. (1968). Is Down's syndrome a modern disease? *Lancet, 2,* 353-354.

Saffran, E.M. & Marin, S.M. (1975). Immediate memory for word lists and sentences in a patient with deficient auditory short-term memory. *Brain and Language, 2,* 420-433.

Salame, P., & Baddeley, A. (1982). Disruption of short-term memory by unattended speech: Implications for the the structure of working memory. *Journal of Verbal Learning and Verbal Behavior, 21,* 150-164.

Schlanger, B.B. & Gottsleben, R.H. (1957). Analysis of speech defects among the institutionalised mentally retarded. *Journal of Speech and Hearing Disorders, 22,* 98-103.

Schweickert, R. & Boruff, B. (1986). Short-term memory capacity: Magic number or magic spell? *Journal of Experimental Psychology: Learning, Memory and Cognition, 12,* 419-425.

Scully, C. (1973). Down's Syndrome. *British Journal of Hospital Medicine, 10,* 89-98.

Segal, S.S. (1967). *No child is ineducable: Special education, provision and trends.* Oxford: Pergamon.

Shallice T. (1989). *From neuropsychology to mental structure.* Cambridge: Cambridge University Press.

Shankweiler, D., & Crain, S. (1986). Language mechanisms and reading disorder: A modular approach. *Cognition, 24,* 139-164.

Simon. H.A. (1974). How big is a chunk? *Science, 183,* 482-488.

Smith, B. & Phillips, C.J. (1981). Age-related progress among children with severe learning difficulties. *Developmental Medicine and Child Neurology, 23,* 465-476.

Snowling M., & Chiat, S. (1990). *Phonological memory and phonological processing: Separate contributions to learning to read?* Paper presented to the Cognitive Neuropsychology Interest Group. London, February 1990.

Snowling, M., Chiat, S., & Hulme, C. (1991). Words, non-words and phonological processes: Some comments on Gathercole, Willis, Emslie and Baddeley. *Applied Psycholinguistics, 12,* 369-373.

Snowling, M., Goulandris, N., Bowlby, M., & Howell, P. (1986). Segmentation and speech perception in relation to reading skill. *Journal of Experimental Child Psychology, 41,* 489-507.

Snowling, M. & Hulme, C. (1989). A longitudinal case study of developmental phonological dyslexia. *Cognitive Neuropsychology, 6,* 379-401.

Snowling, M. & Hulme, C. (in press). Developmental dyslexia and language disorders. In G. Blanken, J. Dittman, H. Grimm, J.C. Marshall, & C.W. Wallesch (Eds.). *Linguistic disorders and pathologies: An international handbook.* New York: De Gruyter.

Snowling, M. & Hulme, C. (in press). Deficits in output phonology: An explanation of reading failure?

Snowling, M., Van Wagtendonk, B., & Stafford, C. (1988). Object naming deficits in developmental dyslexia. *Journal of Research in Reading, 11,* 67-85.

Spreen, O. (1965). Language functions in mental retardation: a review. I. Language development, types of retardation, and intelligence level. *American Journal of Mental Deficiency, 69,* 482-494.

Standing, L., Bond, B., Smith, P., & Isely, C. (1980). Is the immediate memory span determined by sub-vocalisation rate? British Journal of Psychology, 71, 525-539.

Stigler, J.W., Lee S.Y., & Stevenson H.W. (1986). Digit memory in Chinese and English: Evidence for a temporally limited store. *Cognition, 23,* 1-20.

Stratford, B. (1982). Down's syndrome at the Court of Mantua. *Journal of Maternal and Child Health, 7,* 250-254.

Thorley, B. & Wood, V. (1979). Early number experiences for pre-school Down's syndrome children. *Australian Journal of Early Childhealth, 4,* 15-20.

Tizard, J. (1964). *Community Services for the Mentally Handicapped.* Oxford University Press.

Torgeson, J., Rashotte, C., Greenstein J., Houck, G., & Portes, P. (1987). Academic difficulties of learning-disabled children who perform poorly on memory span tasks. In H.L. Swanson (Ed.). *Memory and learning disabilities: Advances in learning and behavioral disabilities.* Greenwich, Conn: JAI Press.

Towbin, A. (1970). Central nervous system damage in the human foetus and newborn infant: mechanical and hypoxic injury, incurred in the foetal neonatal period. *American Journal of Diseases of Children, 119,* 529-542.

Tulving, E. & Donaldson, W. (Eds.) (1972). *Organisation of memory.* New York: Academic Press.

Warnock, M. (1978). *Special educational needs: Report of the Committee of Enquiry into the education of handicapped children and young people.* London: H.M.S.O.

Waters, G., Caplan, D., & Hildebrandt, N. (1987).Working memory and written sentence comprehension. In M. Coltheart (Ed.). *Attention and performance. Vol. 12: The psychology of reading.* Hove: Lawrence Erlbaum Associates Ltd.

Watkins, M.J. (1977). The intricacy of memory span. *Memory and Cognition, 5,* 529-534.

Waugh, N.C. & Norman, D.A. (1965). Primary memory. *Psychological Review, 72,* 89-104.

Weaver, L.A. & Ravaris, C.L. (1970). The distribution of reaction times in mental retardates. *Journal of Mental Deficiency Research, 14,* 295-304.

Wechsler, D. (1976). *Wechsler Intelligence Scale for Children* (Revised) Windsor: NFER.

Woodward, M. (1979). Piaget's theory and the study of mental retardation. In N.R. Ellis (Ed.). *Handbook of mental deficiency, psychological theory and research. (2nd edn).* Hillsdale, N.J.: Lawrence Erlbaum Associates Inc.

World Health Organization (1954). The mentally subnormal child. Technical Rep. Ser, No. 75. Geneva: WHO.

Wright, C.E. (1979). Duration differences between rare and common words and their implications for the interpretation of word frequency effects. *Memory and Cognition, 7,* 411-419.

Zeaman, D. & House, B.J. (1963). The role of attention in retardate discrimination learning. In N. R. Ellis (Ed.). *Handbook of mental deficiency (2nd edn).* Hillsdale, N.J.: Lawrence Erlbaum Associates Inc.

Zeaman, D. & House, B.J. (1979). A review of attention theory. In N.R. Ellis (Ed.). *Handbook of Mental Deficiency 2nd Edition.* Hillsdale, N.J.: Lawrence Erlbaum Associates Inc.

Zhang, G. & Simon, H.A. (1985). STM capacity for Chinese words and idioms: Chunking and acoustical loop hypotheses. *Memory and Cognition, 13,* 193-201.

Author Index

Subject Index